"*The Modern Day Gunslinger* is pure dynamite—a gunfighter's bible. With a fundamental, broad-based foundation of resources, it incorporates the best contributions of the great minds and great trainers in this field. A 'must' for the beginner, the master, or (perhaps most of all) the trainer."

—Lt. Col. David Grossman, author of the Pulitzer
Prize-nominated book *On Killing* and former Army Ranger

"*The Modern Day Gunslinger* should be every shooter's bible! It delivers a straightforward approach to what we all know or knew or should know, setting it straight *as it should be* and serving as a daily reminder of the natural bad habits we all have. It deserves to be on the bedside nightstand to peruse regularly—especially if you don't get to shoot often enough."

—Dick Marcinko, aka Rogue Warrior, Commanding Officer,
SEAL Team SIX, Red Cell (Ret.), and author of over 20 books
including *The New York Times* bestseller *Rogue Warrior*

"Great book! *The Modern Day Gunslinger* should be read by everyone who owns or is considering owning a firearm. Don Mann calls upon his vast experience as a 'shooter' to cover all aspects of shooting but most importantly the mental aspects. He correctly stresses that anyone can shoot at a paper target but not everyone is prepared to shoot at another person in self-defense. This is the best and most concise compendium on weapons defensive tactics I've seen!"

—Robert Gormly, Commanding Officer (Ret.),
SEAL Team TWO and SEAL Team SIX

"*The Modern Day Gunslinger* incorporates real-world survival principles and today's high-speed competition shooting techniques—I highly recommend it to everyone, from novice to seasoned pro. Even if you don't own a firearm, the personal awareness section justifies its purchase."

—Brian Enos, NRA Bianchi Cup and Sportsman's Team Challenge National
Champion Steel Masters Champion, and author of
Practical Shooting—Beyond Fundamentals

"I've been both a student and an instructor of firearms safety, marksmanship and tactics for almost 40 years. During all those years, all those venues, and all the courses attended and conducted, I've never encountered anything that comes as close to saying it all as *The Modern Day Gunslinger* does. I know there will be instructors and students who will be reading MGD for decades to come. This book will save lives."

—Dick Conger, Senior Special Agent (Ret.), U.S. Customs Service, and USG Senior Weapons and Tactics Instructor

"This is the most all-encompassing book on shooting I have ever seen. The complete breakdown of every aspect of combat shooting is meticulously discussed, giving the shooter the concrete fundamentals necessary for fully-developed gunslinger skills. Many how-to manuals try to walk a fine line between covering every detail without boring the reader and trying to hit only the high points to keep the information flowing. Don's writing style has changed the rules altogether. Not only is there a fantastic level of detail, but the facts are presented in a crystal clear fashion, illuminating the fine points in a dynamic approach that allows the reader to enjoy the process and not be intimidated by dry prose. I recommend this book for everybody, whether you are a local shooting champion or a novice who has never held a gun before. If you are even thinking about improving your tactical shooting ability, put all the other books back on the shelf: You have found everything you need in *The Modern Day Gunslinger*."

—Dan Bolchoz, Sergeant Major (Ret.), Delta Force

"Don Mann's book, *The Modern Day Gunslinger*, is a must-read for law enforcement officers, security professionals, military, or civilians wanting to improve their combat firearms skills. Superbly written, comprehensive, and easy-to-understand, this book is a no-nonsense approach to firearms handling, marksmanship, and tactics. Although there are many firearms-related resources on the market, *The Modern Day Gunslinger* contains the most up-to-date and current information in the ever-changing world of combat firearms. I consider this book to be essential reference material and will highly recommend it to my students without reservation."

—Jimmy B., Senior Firearms and Tactics Instructor, USG

"A comprehensive, defensive tactical training guide has been long overdue. Don Mann has filled that gap. *The Modern Day Gunslinger* is an all-inclusive manual that addresses safety, equipment, tactics, and best practices for all shooters. Don and I served together at two different SEAL Commands. I owned an indoor shooting range in Tucson, Arizona, for 10 years and only wish that Don had published this manual then. As an NRA instructor and Arizona Concealed Carry Weapons instructor, I can state emphatically that this manual would have been the only reference my instructors and I would have needed. It would have been mandatory reading for all students."

—Dan T. Coulter, Commander Navy SEAL Team (Ret.)

"As an FBI agent, I have instructed government agents in small arms and tactics from all over the world. *The Modern Day Gunslinger* is an invaluable resource to the FBI and other U.S. government agencies. I have taught firearms, hostage rescue, tactics, and street survival to every level of law enforcement and this book is the only manual that covers every detail of today's gun-fighting issues."

—Roger D. Browning, Special Agent (Ret.),
Federal Bureau of Investigation and USG Senior
Weapons and Tactics Instructor

"Don Mann is an outstanding example of the military men this nation produces, and a top-notch tactical operator and instructor. *The Modern Day Gunslinger* is designed for the novice and expert alike, whose needs range from home defense to government and military missions. It is a very interesting read, chock full of information that may save your life or the life of another. It will have a special place in my library."

—Edward J. Pollard, Assistant Director (Ret.),
Protective Operations, United States Secret Service

"During my 25-year career I worked and trained throughout the world as a government weapons and tactics instructor with the CIA, and as an undercover law enforcement officer. Until now, there has not been a single comprehensive training manual that references all the defensive training and shooting procedures currently taught to the world's most elite military and law enforcement units. *The Modern Day Gunslinger* unlocks the fundamental training secrets in a clear and concise manner, and illuminates a tangible approach to the world of defensive and tactical shooting."

—Jon F., Senior Tactics and Weapons Instructor,
USG

"Don Mann has produced a true quality, top-notch product with his book *The Modern Day Gunslinger*. Don lays it out in layman's terms and covers the whole gambit of shooting skills that build and develop sound shooting techniques from novice to top-notch shooters. Utilizing Don's guidance and skills related in this book, shooters will be able to achieve that higher ability of shooting perfection that will allow them to save lives and be able to return to their loved ones. This is, without a doubt, the most comprehensive, easy-to-read, and understandable instructional shooting book I have ever seen. This is the type of book that will be the milestone on which books on shooting, shooting skills, marksmanship, defensive use of weapons, practical combat applications of weapons, and mind-set will be measured in the future."

—Jim G. Master, Sergeant (Ret.), Special Forces/Ranger/LEO

"Finally, a one-stop source for weapons tactics, techniques, and procedures. I've spent a career in Special Operations, conducting overt, covert, and clandestine operations, learning this all the hard way. Now someone has finally made it simple. Don Mann is a true Quiet Professional. Thanks to him you can simply learn from the best, skip the trial and error, and start concentrating on putting rounds on target."

—Major Luther Papenfus, Major, U.S. Army Special Forces (Ret.)

"A wide-ranging, detailed compendium of the art and philosophy of shooting, written by an experienced SEAL and student of both. This is a *must read* for anyone wishing to understand or master that art."

—Dan'l Steward, Commanding Officer (Ret.), SEAL Team One

"As a chief of law enforcement and firearms instructor, witnessing Don Mann speak and instruct is an extremely motivating experience. His professional, calm, and confident demeanor is a quality that sets Don apart from other weapons and tactics instructors. Students listen and learn—knowing every word spoken is from years of real-world operational experience. I know of no other person who has mastered his craft more expertly, and I know of no better defensive training manual than *The Modern Day Gunslinger*."

—Jan Wright, Chief of Police, Hamburg, New Jersey, Police Department Rc5

"I trained and deployed overseas with Don Mann and have known him well for over 25 years. Don is a world-class weapons and tactics instructor and *The Modern Day Gunslinger* is a testament to Don's knowledge as a weapons instructor. *The Modern Day Gunslinger* is an excellent resource for everyone that has an interest in weapons training—from the military or law enforcement weapons instructor to the novice interested in home defense."

—Randy Goodman, U.S. Navy (SEAL) Captain (Ret.) and Naval Special Warfare Group Commander

"Don Mann is a true warrior. He speaks from a place of knowledge and experience, and has truly 'been there, done that.' By writing *The Modern Day Gunslinger*, he has done an incredible service to the law enforcement, military, and private security communities, not to mention the everyday warriors who understand today's reality: that each one of us is responsible for our own survival."

—Niki Anderson, Counterintelligence Advisor, Centre for Counterintelligence and Security Studies

"During the last 45 years, I have carried a variety of weapons as a combat Marine, a Secret Service Law enforcement Officer, and a USG security contractor. There can be grave legal consequences for anyone improperly carrying or discharging a firearm. My recommendation would be that no one pick up a firearm until they read what Don Mann has written. *The Modern Day Gunslinger* will assist all levels of shooters by presenting clear-cut information covering every aspect of firearm safety and training."

—Bill Wamsley, Deputy Chief (Ret.), U.S. Secret Service

"I personally learned so much from *The Modern Day Gunslinger*, which I consider to be a complete instructional manual for defensive shooting. More importantly, it clearly addresses the responsibility and accountability issues for using a weapon in self-defense. Don Mann addresses the mental aspects that are fundamentally most important in the use of a handgun for self-defense. This book is a terrific tool for beginners and veteran handgun owners who may someday be called to act with a handgun to preserve life, as well as take it. Quite frankly, I found it difficult to put down."

—Dr. Raymond Fritz, Navy SEAL Commander

"The USMC taught me how to use firearms effectively in combat situations. *The Modern Day Gunslinger* builds in depth on this knowledge and experience by clearly discussing safe and effective use of weapons and tactics in civil society, home and personal protection, as well as unusual circumstances. Don Mann's devotion to practicing and teaching these techniques makes this outstanding book a classic in the field. Not only a must-read, but an essential study for any shooter."

—William Davis, PhD, USMC

"*The Modern Day Gunslinger* is a versatile and effective compilation of range safety practices, marksmanship techniques, and combat tactics that will benefit both novice and advanced shooters in many arenas."

—Paul F. Kelly, Firearms Instructor, Special Agent (Ret.),
U.S. Secret Service

"*The Modern Day Gunslinger* is a realistic, practical, easy-to-comprehend manual of the small arms tactics, techniques, and procedures used successfully by our professional and military gunfighters. I recommend this book as an essential reference to anyone committed to perfecting their firearms handling skills."

—John Stann, Captain, USMC

"Don Mann's *The Modern Day Gunslinger* is a concise, practical book on defensive tactical shooting. It is an essential read for anyone from the gun owner interested in home protection to the seasoned military or law enforcement professional. The techniques presented from mind-set and 'survivor's awareness' to marksmanship and then on to tactics is, without doubt, the clearest presentation of defensive shooting I have ever read. This book is highly recommended to anyone interested in seriously improving their shooting skills!"

—Norm Creel, Command Master Chief, SEAL Team Eight

"I believe *The Modern Day Gunslinger* to be an ideal handbook for all shooters. Whether you are a beginner or an advanced shooting professional, there are many lessons and references from which we can all gain. I strongly recommend you pick up a copy of *The Modern Day Gunslinger* for your library; it's well worth it. I give *The MDG* my strongest endorsement."

—Steven W. Bailey, Master Chief, Navy SEAL, USG
Weapons and Tactics Program Manager

THE MODERN DAY GUNSLINGER

THE
MODERN DAY
GUNSLINGER

THE ULTIMATE HANDGUN TRAINING MANUAL

DON MANN, U.S. NAVY SEAL

FOREWORD BY LT. COL DAVID GROSSMAN

Skyhorse Publishing

Skyhorse Publishing books may be purchased in bulk at special discounts for sales promotion, corporate gifts, fund-raising, or educational purposes. Special editions can also be created to specifications. For details, contact the Special Sales Department, Skyhorse Publishing, 307 West 36th Street, 11th Floor, New York, NY 10018 or info@skyhorsepublishing.com.

Skyhorse® and Skyhorse Publishing® are registered trademarks of Skyhorse Publishing, Inc.®, a Delaware corporation.

www.skyhorsepublishing.com

10 9 8 7 6

Library of Congress Cataloging-in-Publication Data

Mann, Don D.
The modern day gunslinger : the ultimate handgun training manual / Don D. Mann.
p. cm.
Includes bibliographical references and indexes.
ISBN 978-1-60239-986-0 (pbk. : alk. paper)
1. Shooting, Military—Handbooks, manuals, etc. 2. Shooting—Handbooks, manuals, etc. 3. Firearms—Handbooks, manuals, etc. I. Title.
UD330.M36 2010
613.6'6--dc22
2010021100

Printed in the United States of America

CONTENTS »

FOREWORD »

Don Devereaux Mann is the real thing, the "right stuff" . . . a Navy SEAL, a combat veteran, and a special operations operator and trainer who has worked, fought beside, and trained the best-of-the-best. Now he has combined his experience and skills to produce a remarkable book, a true gunslinger's textbook . . . a definitive and vital resource.

In the wake of the 9/11 terrorist attacks Americans have risen to the challenge. Many states have established concealed carry laws. Millions of Americans are buying and carrying guns. And if you believe (as I do) that every trained, armed citizen makes America a safer place, then you must believe in this book. Let me say that again: every *trained*, armed citizen. It is not enough to just buy and carry the gun. Now you must train in the use of this vital, lifesaving tool: the handgun. You must strive to become a *Modern Day Gunslinger*.

Consider:

- What is the single most heinous, horrendous international terrorist act in history? What is the single greatest body count, in a single incident, ever achieved by any non-governmental agency not in time of war? The World Trade Center on September 11, 2001 . . .
- What is the single most heinous, horrendous domestic terrorist act in American history, the single greatest body count ever achieved in a terrorist act on American soil by an American Citizen? Oklahoma City . . .
- What is the highest body count of any criminal act on a college campus? Virginia Tech . . .

- What is the single greatest body count ever achieved by any juvenile mass murderer in history? Columbine High School . . .

. . . Not some ancient history. Not some distant land. Us. Now.

There is a new twist to terrorism: It's called body count. Whether the perpetrators are school killers, workplace killers, or international terrorists, they are not interested in negotiating; their only goal is to kill as many people as humanly possible.

Shaken awake by the horror of these events, our citizens and our warriors will no longer sit by as innocent men, women, and children die in helpless mobs. We saw this new thinking on September 11, 2001, when Americans on the fourth airplane, Flight 93 over Pennsylvania, fought back. Americans have determined that they will not be victims!

This is America! Faced with a challenge like this we don't take away rights. We give our citizens more rights! The right to arm and protect ourselves and our loved ones. And, along with that right (as with *any* right) comes responsibility. The responsibility to train and prepare for that fateful day.

It will be extremely difficult for a terrorist to hijack another airplane and fly it into a building. Not just because of all the new security measures, but primarily because any idiot with a box cutter, or any fool who tries to set his shoe on fire, is going to have a planeload of passengers hopping up and down on his body. And if they *do* succeed in hijacking a plane, it will immediately be shot out of the sky by the U.S. Air Force.

No, they will probably not be able to use another plane as a weapon of mass destruction, but what they can do to us is what they have been doing in the Middle East for decades: active shooter strikes. In the Luxor massacre, at the Egyptian tourist site, a handful of armed Islamic extremists gunned down a bunch of tourists. The result was that they shut down the tourism business in Egypt for a year, costing that nation billions of dollars. *This* is the power of the terrorist, be they international or domestic: the ability to shut down a nation with just one strike.

The only viable response to a threat like this is to legally empower, physically arm, and properly train our citizens. *We have been here before.* Take the case of Massachusetts. In 1636, a frustrated General Court of the Massachusetts Bay Colony unanimously passed an ordinance that said:

> "Whereas many complaints have been made to this Court, of the greatest neglect of all sorts of people of using the lawful and necessary means for their safety, especially in this time of so great danger from Indians, it is therefore ordered that no person shall travel above one mile from his dwelling without arms; upon pain of twelve pence for every default."

Being unarmed was considered negligent! Self-protection was not just a personal responsibility, it was a duty to the community! And for over a century after the danger from hostile Indians was eliminated, there was no suggestion that this ordinance be repealed. A century and a half later, those people were the leaders of the armed rebellion that created the United States!

Today Massachusetts has strayed far from its roots. But, as J. R. R. Tolkien put it, in *The Lord of the Rings:*

> All that is gold does not glitter,
> Not all those who wander are lost;
> The old that is strong does not wither,
> Deep roots are not reached by the frost.

Now, in this dark hour, let us tap the strength that is drawn from those deep roots that have endured the bitter frost, let seek out the old that is strong and does not whither, the old ways, the ways of the pioneer and the gunslinger, in order to answer the challenge of the age.

Our forefathers knew that it is not enough to just have a gun, it is also vital to be *trained* in the proper use of that weapon. In 1349, King Edward III of England told the citizens of London that their "skill of shooting" was being neglected, and he proclaimed that "every one of the said city, strong in body, at leisure times on holidays, use in their recreation bow and arrows, or pellets or bolts, and learn and exercise the art of shooting . . . that they do not, after any manner apply themselves to the throwing of . . . handball, football, cambuck, or cockfighting, nor suchlike vain plays which have nor profit in them."

Teddy Roosevelt said, while he was president, that: "We should establish shooting galleries in all the large public and military schools, should maintain national target ranges in different parts of the country, and should in every way encourage the formation of [shooting] clubs throughout all parts of the land . . . It is unfortunately true that the great body of our citizens shoot less and less as time goes on. To meet this [challenge] we should encourage . . . practice . . . by every means in our power. Thus, and not otherwise, may we be able to assist in preserving the peace of the world. Fit to hold our own against the strong nations of the earth, our voice for peace will carry to the ends of the earth. Unprepared and therefore unfit, we must sit dumb and helpless to defend ourselves, protect others, or preserve peace. The first step—to avert war if possible, and to be fit for war if it should come—is to teach our men to shoot."

It bears repeating: our ancestors knew that *it is not enough to just have a gun,* it is also vital to be *trained* in the proper use of that weapon.

And that is what *The Modern Day Gunslinger* is all about. Here, in your hands, is one of the finest defensive weapons training resources available. If you have doubts about the things recommended in this book, simply try them yourself. I have, and I can tell you that they work.

A true master, a world class shooter, operator and weapons and tactics trainer has turned his remarkable skills toward teaching you to properly employ defensive handgun tactics when required. I strongly recommend that you not just read but study and apply this excellent book.

—Dave Grossman
Lt. Col., U.S. Army (ret.)
Author of *On Killing* and *On Combat*
President, Warrior Science Group (www.WarriorSci.com)

Cogito, ergo armatum sum.
I think, therefore I am armed.

INTRODUCTION »

Before getting into the defensive and tactical training techniques involved with shooting, we should first go over why the information you'll find in these pages matters.

During my career, expanding close to thirty-five years, I have worked with and learned from some of the most talented shooters in the world. I have also learned that some of the best disagree with one another. And that perplexed me: How can one shooting instructor, with IPSC titles, victorious in gun battles all over the world, so vehemently disagree with another with similar credentials? More often than not, the answer lies in the medium through which each shooter has acquired his expertise. There is a big difference between shooting on a range at two-dimensional paper targets, and training with methods that work when the targets are firing back at you. However, when you combine these experiences and bounce their lessons off each other, what you get is a wide-ranging, even humbling perspective on weaponry and shooting itself.

In preparing the *MDG*, I corresponded with many of the big names in the shooting world. Most of them graciously agreed to share their wisdom. I also read all I could find on shooting, part of a research process that has taken over twelve years. My expertise alone wasn't enough to inform you in the comprehensive manner that was my intent.

My work and research, I hope, presents a balanced look at what the professional shooters have to say, what those in law enforcement have to say, and what military personnel who have fought in combat have to say about what works and doesn't work.

As such, the shooting skills taught in the *MDG* carry broad application in civilian, law enforcement and military contexts. We all need to prepare for worst-case scenarios. Common criminals, terrorists, assailants—the enemy and threat—all will find themselves outgunned in the face of a properly armed and trained gunslinger. Members of the armed services, government and law enforcement agencies, as well as civilians will find that the close-range shooting methods addressed herein can provide a decisive advantage.

Before we get too far, however, remember this: I don't claim to be all-knowing. As a matter of fact, I am far from it. I am a weapons and tactics professional and have a great deal of respect and admiration for those who treat weapons and weapons training with the respect they deserve. I am a retired Navy SEAL and a U.S. Government Small Arms and Tactics instructor, jobs for which I have operated and traveled around the world and have trained civilian and military personnel, foreign leaders and heads of state protection details.

I have developed many focused small-arms training and tactics courses, manuals, and lesson plans for the U.S. military and U.S. government. Like those manuals, this book explains technical and non-technical information on the defensive use of handguns. It also breaks down weapons safety, basic shooting fundamentals, ammunition, low-light and no-light shooting, holsters, and "combat mindset"—a mental approach to everyday life that plays an important role in a gunslinger's effectiveness.

Nevertheless, the information you'll find herein is intended only as a complement to the rest of the shooting expertise available in our field. I encourage all readers of this text to digest all they feel relevant to their own lives and professions, and then go further and learn and train with a professional shooter or shooting academy.

Like most weapons instructors, I am and always will remain a student first, an instructor second—I will never know all there is to know on this subject. And it often worries and frustrates me when I come across an instructor who has an answer for *every* situation. In my mind, no such person exists.

But we can try to come close. This book was written to meet the needs of: the gun owner; the experienced shooter; those who own a weapon strictly for home- and self-defense; for the military member who wants to become a better shooter in defense of our country; for the law enforcement officer who risks his or her life going against the thugs of our society; and for anyone interested in learning the defensive and tactical training techniques from some of the best and most experienced shooters in the world.

My "professional" shooting career began soon after I joined the Navy. I spent 21 years in the Navy, most of it with the SEAL teams, some of it with the Marine Corps. I spent another 10 years as a small arms and tactics instructor with the government. I always felt confident and competent when it came to weapons handling, marksmanship, and combat shooting—though initially, I never thought there was much more I needed to know about weapons training. After all, I was a SEAL and I could shoot, move, and communicate with the best of them.

Well, I was wrong. There was a lot I did not know. In 1983 a few of us from SEAL Team One had the opportunity to attend Gunsite, one of the world's first and finest shooting academies, and have the legendary Colonel Jeff Cooper personally teach our .45-caliber tactical pistol course. At the time, I didn't fully appreciate just how vast an influence this great man would have on me and the shooting world in general. But he shaped us all to some degree, having taught many of the instructors who now teach the students and instructors of today.

Prior to Jeff Cooper, other premier shooting and tactics gurus included Colonel Rex Applegate and Bill Jordan. Much of the early documented studies and research stem from the works of these men. In an ode to the unending evolution you see in the shooting world, however, even their findings are now often criticized and debated among some of today's top shooters, well-known small arms and tactics scholars and instructors, and IPSC/IDPA champions.

Applegate, Jordan, and Cooper didn't see eye-to-eye on weapons or tactical training techniques. Nor do today's big names in the shooting community, among them Doug Koenig, Rob Leatham, Ron Avery, John Shaw, and Massad Ayoob—to name just a few.

In my opinion, there needs to be a definitive source of information that discusses why certain defensive tactics are used. It is important for us all to know, as students, that some tactics and techniques may work some of the time, others work other times, but none of them work all of the time. In the SEAL teams we often would say that "situation dictates" when to use what you have in your toolbox. It is a "thinking man's game" and you may have a very short amount of time to decide what tactic or procedure you think will work best in your given situation.

I often tell shooters that I do not like to use the word "never" or the word "always," because at some point in time I will be incorrect. I cannot tell a student that he must always take cover in a gunfight, because in some situations, the best tactic may be to draw down on the threat as quickly as possible and shoot until that threat has been neutralized. There may be no time to "take cover"; the closest cover may be one hundred yards away.

Over 25 years I accumulated unquantifiable depths of information on shooting: from my own experiences, lessons from the professionals, military and law enforcement personnel, not to mention videos, magazines, books, notes from the pros, shooting classes, and shooting schools. The goal—to create a very comprehensive shooting training manual that would be of great value to the military, the law enforcement community, and to those keen on home- and self-defense. It was during my research that I realized a comprehensive defensive handgun shooting manual did not exist. There were many great sources of information available, many outstanding books from the best in the shooting community, and many Web sites devoted to shooting and tactics education—but there was not a comprehensive defensive tactical training manual.

After weeding out the irrelevant, the redundant, the obsolete and the ridiculous from the stockpiles of information I had, this project was shaping up into something along the lines of what I envisioned and something I was very proud of. But it was far from complete. Although I had my own experiences and training, the military perspective, the law enforcement perspective and the civilian's perspective, I lacked substantial material from those who really studied the art and science of shooting. I lacked the expertise and points of view of the top professional shooters in the United States, people who make a living as modern day gunslingers.

Most competitive IPSC and IDPA shooters shoot at paper and steel, which, of course, do not shoot back. Many of them use "race guns"—which the rest of the shooting community does not use—and many of the rules in competition differ from those on the streets, in combat, the convenience store robbery, etc. However, these competitive shooters can teach us a great deal on weapons handling, and fast and accurate shooting. These gunslingers have studied and broken down every aspect of shooting to an infinitesimal degree convenient for our benefit, in this case. And, many of the IPSC and IDPA top guns are law enforcement officers or military personnel who have stood face-to-face with deadly threats.

Other than competitions in the SEAL teams, I have done little competitive shooting in my lifetime. I always considered myself a combat shooter, not a sport shooter. But, as most combat shooters or recreational shooters will tell you, some of what we were taught came from the professional competition shooters. They know how to shoot faster than the eye can follow, and they always move with purpose and great efficiency.

I had literally thousands of opportunities to learn from these same people—shooters who are, quite simply, the best in the world. I consulted them even further so as to incorporate their knowledge into this book. It was a critical addition, one that finally began to round out the balance of expertise.

When we start to apply the information in the chapters that follow, it's important to keep in mind one sobering truth: We are living in a very dangerous time. Our children attend schools in environments that have become unpredictable, even deadly in many instances. When I was growing up, I never had to worry about my classmates carrying a weapon to school. Today it is a way of life.

To survive in this world, you don't need to be the one pounding your chest showing everyone just how capable, tough, and ready you are. Be the silent warrior instead—the modern day gunslinger. Keep it to yourself, but be confident with your skills. Let it become part of your mind-set. Hopefully you will never need the defensive skills discussed in this book, but just think how terrible you would feel if you or your family needed them and you were not ready to use them.

Shooting Maxims

"War is an ugly thing, but not the ugliest of things; the decayed and degraded state of moral and patriotic feeling which thinks that nothing is worth war is much worse. A man who has nothing for which he is willing to fight, nothing he cares about more than his own personal safety, is a miserable creature who has no chance of being free, unless made and kept so by the exertions of better men than himself."

—John Stuart Mill

"Honor never grows old, and honor rejoices the heart of age. It does so because honor is, finally, about defending those noble and worthy things that deserve defending, even if it comes at a high cost. In our time, that may mean social disapproval, public scorn, hardship, persecution, or as always, even death itself."

—William J. Bennett

WEAPONS AND RANGE SAFETY

Weapons Safety

Before we discuss weapons, training and ammunition, it's only right that we go over all facets of weapons safety. Safety, after all, means freedom from danger. It's critical to recognize and respect the

Range training gear

significance of safety when it comes to owning and operating fire-arms. There are generally two major reasons that people are inadvertently shot—ignorance and carelessness.

Becoming a safe shooter should always be your main priority. It would do you little good to learn to shoot a weapon and accidentally wound or kill a family member or a fellow shooter. Unfortunately this happens far too often—but it would not happen at all if everyone followed the simple list of shooting rules.

You really cannot afford to make a mistake while handling fire-arms. There are safety rules you need to adhere to whenever handling weapons. Every time you go to the range to shoot, you should review these rules.

It was the great Colonel Cooper who developed the basic weapons safety rules most universally adopted by most civilian, law enforcement, government, and military ranges and weapons instructors. You can find these rules at most ranges. Many instructors, shooting

Range training gear

Loaded AK-47s

doctrines and various ranges have modified the colonel's works, but the following four basic rules still apply today.

Four Rules of Safety

Safety Rule #1

Always treat all weapons as if they are loaded.

The chances are that someday the "unloaded" gun you pick up will be loaded, and this can prove to be catastrophic. The majority of people who have been shot unintentionally have been shot with firearms that were presumed to be unloaded. That's why we treat every firearm as if it's loaded. "I didn't know the gun was loaded" is a pitiful excuse for accidentally killing or seriously injuring another human being. When you pick up a gun, visually and physically check the weapon twice. Every time you pick up the weapon check its condition. You have to be 100 percent certain of the condition of the weapon.

Always check weapon twice, visually and physically,
to ensure you have an empty weapon.

Press-check to ensure a round has been chambered.

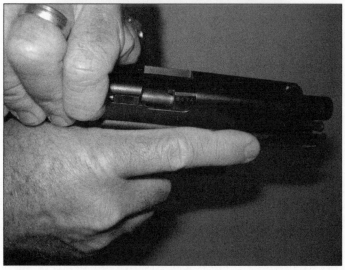

When you check a weapon, be sure to keep it pointed in a safe direction. If you want an unloaded (semi) weapon, always remove the magazine first—"remove the source." Then rack the slide to the rear two or three times and keep it locked to the rear. Visually and physically check (with the tip of your finger) the chamber and the magazine well; then look away for a moment's pause, before checking it a second time. It is important to do the physical check, because in low-light and no-light situations, you will not be able to see if the weapon is loaded.

Often times a student will ask, "Why should I check my weapon twice?" The answer is simple. Have you ever looked at your watch and not noticed what time it is? You have to look a second time to actually register what you are seeing.

If your intent is to have a loaded (semi) weapon, conduct a "press check." With your weapon pointed down range or in a safe direction, partially pull the slide to the rear until you can see the round, yet being careful not to eject the round. Be sure not to sweep your hand in front of the muzzle during the press check.

Never underestimate your weapon's potential to be loaded—especially if it is ever out of your control. You are responsible for every round that is fired from your weapon.

Safety Rule #2

Never allow the muzzle to cross anything you're not prepared to destroy.

Don't be careless with how you handle a weapon. *Always* keep the weapon pointed in a safe (or the safest possible) direction. A safe direction means that the weapon is pointed so that even if it were to go off, it would not cause injury or damage to anyone or anything you would not want to destroy. The key to this rule is to control where the muzzle is pointed at all times.

To do so, imagine there is a powerful laser beam being emitted from the muzzle and that anything swept by the muzzle will be destroyed.

In a real encounter, it's possible that a shooter will laser a non-threat or even his fellow shooters. There's no firing line on the street or the battlefield, and there will undoubtedly be innocents downrange when you need to shoot.

Although it is wrong and should never occur, many shooters laser themselves while reholstering. Many shooters, as well as some instructors, angle the weapon in toward their body while holstering the weapon in the strong-side holster. In doing so, these shooters may actually laser their abdomen, pelvis, and thigh.

There are numerous accidents each year related to people shooting themselves while reholstering. Second Chance Body Armor offers a Kevlar holster as a direct result of the number of law enforcement officers who shoot themselves while reholstering. Keep in mind most of these officers who accidentally shot themselves would not have done so if their fingers had not been on the trigger (Safety Rule #3). While drawing a weapon out of a strong-side holster, there is a natural upward and forward momentum. Returning the weapon to the holster, however, is a slower movement that requires you to crank your shoulder up into a chicken-wing position. This motion is uncomfortable for many of us—and larger people and those with limited flexibility have an even harder time doing it. Sometimes shooters avoid this discomfort by raising their shoulders as little as possible. The less you raise your shoulder the easier it is to angle the muzzle toward your body, if you're not careful.

Look around when you're handling a weapon and always consider the bullet's potential path. You must not permit that muzzle projection to cross anything that you can't justify shooting. This must become a trained, subconscious behavior if a shooter is to be truly safe with a firearm.

Safety Rule #3

Keep your finger off the trigger until your sights are on the target and you have made the conscious decision to shoot.

Never place your finger on the trigger until you are ready to fire your weapon. It is close to impossible for a gun in your hand to fire if your finger doesn't come in contact with the trigger, although there are times when the trigger can get caught up on clothing or gear. Yet this is the hardest rule for shooters to follow for a couple of reasons: many people feel that firearms are designed to be held with the finger on the trigger and nearly everyone who has grown up in modern society has been bombarded with photos, movies, and TV programs where actors are routinely pictured with their fingers on the triggers.

If the finger is placed on the front of the trigger guard, rather than alongside the frame of the weapon, the reaction of clenching the fist can result in an unintended discharge as the finger snaps off the finger guard toward the waiting trigger. Never touch the trigger, or even let your finger enter the trigger guard unless your sights are on target and you have made the conscious decision to shoot.

Weapons don't discharge by themselves, except in very rare instances (e.g., cookoffs). Inevitably, if the weapon fired, it was because the trigger was pulled.

Do not place all of your trust in a mechanical safety; as with any mechanical device, it is subject to failure. A straight trigger finger is the only real safety, so keep it that way—long and straight—until you're ready to shoot.

Neurological reactions that account for the "startle response":

In a stressful situation, when you get startled your extremities will tighten. If the finger is on the trigger or within the trigger guard when any of these neurological responses take place, an accidental discharge can occur.

The startle response will also occur for the following reasons:

- Postural Instability: When the shooter slips, loses balance, or begins to fall, his hands will react and tighten.
- Overflow Effect: When utilizing the non-shooting hand, for any reason, and it tightens to some extent, the shooting hand will tighten.

Note: The "reaction to shoot" time is no different with the finger on or off the trigger; therefore it is safer to keep the finger straight alongside the slide or receiver, since it does not put the shooter at a disadvantage.

Safety Rule #4

Be sure of your target and what is beyond and adjacent to the target.

Along the same lines of the first three safety rules, there is absolutely no excuse for shooting at an unidentified target, namely anything you have not identified as a threat. That means you never fire at a human silhouette or shadow, just like you never fire at a sound (the battlefield is a different story since often you end up firing at muzzle flashes). You are responsible for every round that leaves your weapon, be it an intended target or unintended target.

This does not mean that we cannot take a shot on the streets unless the threat is standing in front of a berm or brick wall. But it does mean we must strike our intended target. You do not want a stray round to injure or kill innocent people. Unfortunately, most threats do not worry about this since they just fire at will.

Think of it this way: There are never misses, only unintended targets. Every bullet hits something.

A shooter must only shoot when he is certain he will hit his target. When beyond the range of a certain hit due to distance, angle, or amount of light, one should hold his fire and withdraw, or advance to cover if possible. Shooters must make their own decisions about when to fire. The shooting decision involves not only the actions of the threat but the shooter's self-assessment of his ability under the circumstances. Be absolutely sure you have identified your target beyond any doubt and be aware of the area beyond and adjacent to your target.

A Matter of Life and Death

All too often, we read about the tragic loss of an innocent life because of improperly stored firearms. Many of these accidents, suicides, and injuries are preventable when firearms are properly stored.

Parents and care givers can help prevent such tragedies by safeguarding weapons from children. The way in which weapons are stored can be a matter of life and/or accidental death. Approximately 75 percent of all firearm-related accidents and suicides involving children and teens, as well as many homicides and injuries, are committed with a firearm found at home, or the home of a relative or friend.

A responsible adult cannot rely on a young child, teenager, or adult not to touch a weapon merely because they have been told not to do so. It is impossible to predict what others will do, and the risks of mishandling a weapon are too great to place the burden of responsibility on anyone other than the adult bringing the weapon into the home.

Nevertheless, gun owners have a responsibility to talk with their family about the dangers of weapons. If possible teach weapons safety and teach them how to shoot. Family members need to be told in no uncertain terms that they are not allowed to touch the weapons unless properly trained and or supervised.

Gun owners have a responsibility to maintain control of their weapons via proper storage, handling, and operation at all times. It is not only a law in some states for gun owners to ensure weapons are stored properly, but it is our obligation to our family and to our society to keep weapons out of the hands in which they do not belong. In most U.S. jurisdictions, gun owners who fail to take "reasonable precautions" to restrict access to their firearms will most likely be held accountable in civil court for damage caused by them.

Range Safety

Eye & Ear Protection

A shooting range is a specialized facility designed specifically for firearms training. Each facility is typically overseen by a range master. Although these supervisory personnel are "responsible" for ensuring that all weapons safety and range rules are followed at the range, safety and range rules are ultimately every shooter's responsibility to follow.

Sight and hearing protection are essential anytime weapons are being fired. Whether indoors or outdoors, all shooters are required to wear safety goggles or glasses, as well as hearing protection (hard ear protection and/or earplugs) at all times when within the defined boundaries of the range.

A pair of proper-fitting shooting glasses or goggles, in good condition, should protect the shooter from ejected cases, dirt or target ricochets, unburned powder granules, or droplets of hot oil that can come off the rear of the slides of the semis.

Earplugs will reduce the level of noise traveling through the ear canal, but with most weapons and shooting environments the shooting noises are loud enough that they travel through the bone to the inner ear often causing irreversible hearing loss. When possible wear both soft ear protection and hard ear protection. I do not know of a shooting instructor or a shooter who has been shooting for a significant period of time who does not have significant hearing loss.

Children are even more vulnerable to hearing loss than adults.

Lead Dangers & Contamination

When I first started shooting, we would pick up our brass, place it into our ballcaps, dump the brass into the garbage, place our ballcaps back on our heads, and then go eat. We never considered this brass contained lead and that the lead from the hats should not go on our heads; nor did we think about washing our hands after shooting, before eating, etc. Unfortunately, many shooters from my generation, as well as those before us, are now suffering or have suffered from lead poisoning. Recent studies on lead poisoning from shooting are shocking and have fortunately resulted in things being done quite differently now.

When shooting lead ammunition, small amounts of lead are vaporized into the air. This vapor condenses to fine, potentially lethal particles. These particles are inhaled and absorbed into the body and eventually dissolve in stomach acid, which allows this toxic lead to enter our blood supply.

Repeated exposure of lead ingestion/respiration produces lead toxicity, which affects most of the body's organs. When lead makes its way into the bone, it persists even longer in the body.

Leave your shooting clothing and footwear at the range or somewhere outside of the home or workplace. Do not bring these deadly particles into your home or workplace where they will find their way into your clothing, bedding, carpeting, and upholstery and continue to find their way into your body and into those around you for many years.

Remember, you are exposed to lead every time you step on a range, handle or clean a firearm, sweep or pick up brass, or handle targets.

If you shoot often, you should get annual blood tests. The average person has about 6 micrograms of lead per deciliter of blood. If the levels reach 20–30 μg/dL you are subject to physiological problems. If over 80 μg/dL, the damage is likely to be serious and permanent. The effects on children are even more debilitating.

Bore Obstructions

One of the most common causes of catastrophic failure of any firearm occurs when two rounds collide in the barrel. This can rupture the barrel, the dust cover, and possibly the frame and slide of the weapon. The effect of an obstruction can be anywhere from barely noticeable to devastating.

Before you load your weapon, open the action and make certain it is empty. Visually and physically check the weapon twice to be sure the barrel is clear of any obstruction. Even a small bit of dirt, mud, snow, or excess lubricating oil in the bore can result in dangerously increased pressures, and cause the barrel to bulge or even burst on firing, which can seriously injure the shooter and bystanders.

Make it a habit to inspect and clean the bore with a cleaning rod and patch to wipe away anti-rust compounds in the weapon each time before you shoot. If the noise or recoil on firing seems weak or not quite right, cease firing immediately and be sure to check that an obstruction or projectile has not become lodged in the barrel.

Safe Storage and Operation

When you own and handle weapons, you assume a great responsibility. Weapons can unintentionally result in death or serious injury if used carelessly or improperly.

As mentioned earlier, all weapons must be kept secure from unauthorized or untrained individuals, be they your children, your spouse, neighbors, or criminals. That may involve locking up the firearms, the ammunition, or both. To help solve this problem, there are some lockboxes on the market to keep weapons fairly secure, yet quickly accessible.

Good safety habits must be cultivated to the point where they are part of your mind-set. Here are a few of the most important:

- *Be sure the weapon is safe to operate.* Weapons require periodic maintenance, regular cleaning, and proper storage. If there are questions concerning a weapon's ability to function, consult a knowledgeable shooter or gunsmith.
- *Use only the recommended ammunition.* Many weapons have the ammunition type stamped on the barrel. Ammunition can be identified by information printed on the container and sometimes stamped on the cartridge. Do not shoot the weapon unless you are certain you have the proper ammunition.
- *Never use alcohol or mind-altering drugs, be they over-the-counter or prescription, before or while shooting.* There is a zero-tolerance policy against the use of alcohol and any other substances known to impair normal mental or physical bodily functions when handling weapons.

- *Secure weapons so they are not accessible to unauthorized persons.* Numerous gun storage and locking devices that attach to weapons are available. However, mechanical locking devices, like the mechanical safeties built into weapons, can fail and should not be used as a substitute for safe gun handling and storage. Also keep in mind, however, that if a weapon is to be used for defense, it does not make sense to keep a lock on it, as it needs to be quickly available to the shooter.

Weapons Cleaning

Regular cleaning is important in order for your weapon to operate correctly and safely. Taking proper care of your weapon will maintain its value and extend its life. A weapon brought out of prolonged storage should always be cleaned and function-checked before operating. Accumulated moisture, sweat, dirt, solidified grease, gun lubricant, and oil, can prevent the weapon from operating properly. Before cleaning your weapon, be sure it is unloaded. And be sure that ammunition is not present in the cleaning area.

Range Commands

There are many different variations of range commands, but in this text I list only the most common. The commands that follow are what I use when training U.S. and foreign military and government personnel. These commands are simple, short, and although used in an administrative and training environment, parallel tactical steps as well.

Once you have your mind free of distractions and all of your shooting gear ready (i.e., hat, ear and eye protection, holster, ammo, and weapon) step up to the line. Once up to the line, you should be given the command to draw or "come to the ready," then "check your weapon, both visually and physically to ensure you have a safe and empty weapon." The next command may be "with a full magazine, load, press-check, and holster" or "load, press-check, and come to the ready."

Once the range master has seen that everyone appears ready to shoot, you will hear some variation of "ready on the right, ready on the left, the firing line is ready." Next will be the command "stand-by—up!"

"Ready" typically means to come to the ready position.

With pistols, your weapon is pointed down range, you have acquired a good two-handed high grip, your elbows are indexed into your ribs, and your shooting finger is straight alongside the frame of the pistol. Your stance is correct and your mind is 100 percent focused on the task at hand. If your weapon has an external safety, many ranges allow you to take it off safe at this position.

"Up" means to punch your weapon straight out toward the target and shoot as directed by the range master, for example "two shots center mass" or "Mozambique."

"Follow-through" and "scan" should happen automatically. These should not be a range command although some range masters verbalize this command until they see that the shooters do it on their own.

"With a straight finger—holster." If your weapon has a safety you will safe the weapon and then holster. Be sure not to sweep your body when holstering.

Shooting Maxims

"A citizen who shirks his duty to contribute to the security of his community is little better than the criminal who threatens it."

"Policemen are nobody's personal bodyguards. Their jobs are to find and arrest people who have committed crimes, not to prevent such potential crimes from happening in the first place. Clearly, the responsibility for victim-prevention lies with the victim-to-be."

"'Liberty or death,' the meaning of which is clear and absolute, is but a trivial phrase if you do not carry a gun. For freedom-loving Americans, the five most important words in the English language are, and always have been—from my cold dead hands."

"Remember, our liberty is protected by four boxes: The Ballot Box, The Jury Box, The Soap Box, and The Cartridge Box." Our freedom is real simple when put in proper context. Remove one, the rest will fall."

"No free man shall ever be debarred the use of arms."

—Thomas Jefferson

"The strongest reason for the people to retain the right to keep and bear arms is, as a last resort, to protect themselves against tyranny in government."

—Thomas Jefferson

"Arms discourage and keep the invader and plunderer in awe, and preserve order in the world as well as property . . . Horrid mischief would ensue were the law-abiding deprived of the use of them."

—Thomas Paine, 1775

"Firearms stand next in importance to the Constitution itself. They are the American people's liberty, teeth and keystone under independence . . . From the hour the Pilgrims landed to the present day, events, occurrences, and tendencies prove that to insure peace, security, and happiness, the rifle and pistol are equally indispensable. . . . The very atmosphere of firearms anywhere and everywhere restrains evil interference—they deserve a place of honor with all that's good. . . ."

—Attributed to George Washington

DRY FIRE

Dry fire training can be very beneficial in many ways for any shooter. It allows the shooter to become more familiar with his weapon and weapon handling skills such as drawing, holstering, and reloading. It has also proven to be very helpful in preventing the development of a flinch or curing an existing one, since it can rid the aversive stimuli of the shot going off.

Dry fire is often more convenient than going to the range. It allows you to practice basic weapon handling skills pretty much anywhere. You can train at home, for instance, and in a few hours you can practice hundreds of repetitions for attaining perfect sight alignment, perfect trigger control, follow-through, and scanning, in addition to the skills mentioned above. You can also practice: shooting from behind cover; tactical and speed reloads; and correcting malfunctions, all in various shooting positions, such as prone, kneeling supported, kneeling unsupported, and standing.

Dry fire is something every serious shooter incorporates into his training. The Marine Corps spends countless hours perfecting its riflemen's skills through dry fire. I cannot emphasize how important dry fire is to anyone who owns and handles weapons.

Dry fire training

Unfortunately, dry fire can also be very dangerous. Many people have been seriously wounded or killed through "dry fire." Many accidental shootings are caused by someone failing to follow the basic safety rules, namely ensuring the weapon is unloaded.

Still, dry fire is easily done safely. When dry fire training, go through all the motions of handling the weapon as though it were live fire: check the weapon twice—both visually and physically—and follow the four safety rules. Additionally, there are rules specific to dry fire that must be followed as well.

The Dry Fire Safety Ritual

The dry fire ritual must be done the same way every time. Just like all other weapons training, this safe dry fire ritual has to become hard-wired into the shooter's subconscious.

Never allow interruptions during this ritual. Do not have TV or music playing and turn off all phones. Ensure your dry fire area is secure by keeping the door locked so people cannot walk in during your training.

This dry fire ritual cannot be interrupted. If it is, begin the ritual all over from step one. The dry fire ritual:

- Check to make sure that the weapon is unloaded. Check weapon twice, both visually and physically. If you have a revolver, run your finger across the opening to each chamber in the cylinder. Count the empty holes to be sure you checked them all.
- Keep all ammunition out of the room and out of sight. Lock the door to the room where the ammunition is kept so that it takes several deliberate steps to get it.
- Select a safe backstop. If you do not have a reliable backstop do not dry fire. (Remember Safety Rule #4: Know your target and what is behind it.) You will need a backstop that would actually stop a handgun round. You must be certain that an unintended shot could not possibly do any harm other than minor property damage. Furniture, TVs, doors, interior walls, dry walls, and standard exterior walls (unless made from solid brick) generally do not stop handgun rounds.

Safe handgun round stops include:
» Two-to-three-foot-thick stack of phone books. Many shooters place a stack of phone books inside a cardboard box. After dry fire practice is over, take the phone books out of the box and keep the box out of sight until the next dry firing session.
» A bookshelf filled with books leaving no space between the books, will stop a handgun round if you fire from the long end of the bookshelf. Aim at the bookcase end, so an unexpected bullet would travel the entire length of the bookshelf before coming to rest somewhere between the pages.

» A brick fireplace or a cement wall but there is a ricochet potential.

» Body armor or a bullet-resistant vest

» A five gallon bucket of sand.

» Obviously, any or all of these things will result in property damage if you accidentally shoot them. The bulletproof vest, for example, would subsequently be useless. Replacing the books could be quite an ordeal. And repairing brick or cement walls is somewhat difficult. However minor property damage is acceptable—uncontained bullets are not. Always be sure your weapon is unloaded!

Tape a target to the backstop and immediately remove the target before reloading. Never leave the target up after reloading. That way you won't be tempted to take "just one more shot," forgetting that the weapon is loaded. Put the target away, out of sight, before you get the ammunition out of the other room and before you reload.

Commence dry fire training. If at any time you lose your focus or your ability to concentrate, it is time to take a break or stop dry firing. When you cannot give your full undivided attention, safety is compromised.

"I wholeheartedly recommend dry fire practice. I attribute dry fire to my ability to classify as master in several disciplines within a year after I first started shooting. When you dry fire, you can practice just about any of the skills you can work on in live fire without going to the range and paying for targets, ammo, or range time. Then when you do go to the range, you only have to verify the dry fire practice has helped you to become proficient at the basic skills. Generally, after the first few weeks of practice, I recommend you dry fire at least weekly and shoot live-fire at least monthly."

—Robbie Robinson

USE OF FORCE

Legally, you have a right to defend yourself as long as you haven't provoked the confrontation. If you are armed, you are expected to take particular care to avoid a fight that may result in the *use of force*. You generally are not allowed to use a greater level of force than that force which threatens you.

Deadly Force

Deadly force is defined as the force with which a reasonable person, knowing what he knows at the time, could reasonably expect to kill or cause grave bodily harm.

Different states have specific definitions, particularly of "grave bodily harm," "great bodily injury," "serious bodily injury," etc. *Grave bodily harm* generally refers to crippling injuries. In some jurisdictions it is also known as *great bodily injury*.

If you are forced to defend yourself with deadly force, it should be the threat that makes the decision for you. You will never be required by law to give up your own life instead of employing enough force to kill the threat. On that note, if an assailant threatens you in such a manner, he is basically giving you the legal right to end his life. You must use that right.

That said, you may use deadly force only in the event of an *immediate* and otherwise *unavoidable* threat of death or grave bodily harm.

If someone angrily bolts away from a fight and promises to return to finish what he started by killing you later, the threat is not *immediate*. Likewise, if someone openly offers you time to escape, the threat is *avoidable*.

If the attack is an attempt to take your weapon, then recovering your weapon must be your first priority. If the up-close attack is made by a threat holding a weapon, then disarming him may be the appropriate response.

If you are reasonably in fear for your life and cannot escape, then the use of deadly force may be justified.

As defensive firearms expert Stephen Wenger writes, "The decision to use deadly force, upon recognition that someone is trying to kill or seriously injure you, must be made in advance. Once the threat occurs you will not have the time to make that moral decision; your mind needs to be free for the best possible assessment of the threat and the choice of tactics.

"In order for the law to accept your shooting another human being, he must have placed you in reasonable fear for your life or that of another innocent person. The emphasis is on 'reasonable.' If the fear becomes an overwhelming emotion it can interfere with both your reasoning and your function."

There are many reasons why deadly force might be necessary. Among them are:
- There are multiple threats.
- The threat is armed.
- There is a disparity in size, strength, and/or age between the defender and the threat.
- The threat is high on alcohol or drugs such as PCP, crack, or meth.
- The threat has a history of violence.

- The threat has specialized skills, such as martial arts training.
- The threat is attempting to disarm the defender.

Ability, Opportunity, and Jeopardy

The very moment you are confronted by a threat possessing the *intent, ability,* and *opportunity* to cause serious bodily harm or death—and you feel you life is in jeopardy—you should immediately do whatever it takes to neutralize the threat. I am not discussing specific legalities here since I am not an attorney and laws vary from state to state. As a shooter, you need to be aware of the laws that govern your state.

As a defensive shooter, you are not permitted to preemptively strike or go on the offense. So since you will be the target of the threat you will almost always start out at a distinct disadvantage in terms of your ability to react. The threat will have the advantage. The threat does not worry about state laws, use of force policy or fighting fair. And action is always quicker than reaction. Your reaction must be quick and effective and seconds will seem like an eternity.

More and more often, we are faced with multiple threats. One law enforcement study showed that the average number of threats an officer had to confront at once was 1.5. This highlighted the fact that training had to include how to effectively engage multiple threats.

The Federal Bureau of Investigation (FBI) determined that the shootings their agents are involved in more closely approximate civilian defensive scenarios. From 1989 through 1994, the majority of FBI shooting incidents allegedly took place at a distance of 6–10 feet (approx. 2–3 meters), with roughly 40 percent of the incidents taking place at distances exceeding 21 feet (approx. 7 meters). The breakdown is as follows:

- 0–20 feet 60 percent of the time
- 21–45 feet 30 percent of the time
- 46–75 feet 10 percent of the time
  . . . And never beyond 75 feet.

When confronted by a threat you must quickly determine whether the threat possesses the *intent, ability,* and *opportunity* to cause you serious bodily harm or death—"jeopardy." Because of the short distances involved and time consumed by decision making, the ability to strike your threat effectively is simply a matter of your life or death.

If you use lethal force, in order for you to claim that you were reasonably in fear for your life, or the lives of others you had a right to protect, the following three conditions must be legally met:

Ability

The threat must possess the *ability* to kill or cause grave bodily harm. This can be broadly interpreted and does not simply mean the threat has a weapon capable of maiming another person. The threat might also be 6-foot-5 and 300 pounds of muscle, or a professional boxer. These characteristics enable the threat to inflict harm on a different scale than would an average human being.

Opportunity

Dennis Tueller developed what is now known as the "21-foot rule," which is often cited in court. The threat must have the opportunity to employ his ability. For example, a man with a knife who is on the other side of a busy four-lane highway doesn't have the opportunity to kill or maim you with a knife, but he does with a firearm.

An unarmed group threatening to kill you from behind a ten-foot-high chain link fence lacks the opportunity, even though they have the ability. The assailant must have the *opportunity* to employ their ability at 21 feet. If someone is attacking you from 21 feet with a knife, he can be on you in 1.5 seconds, according to Tueller's research. A person threatening you with a knife, from this distance, with no obstacles in the way, has both the *ability* and the *opportunity.* Tueller states that a man can run 21 feet in about 1.5 seconds (75 feet/25 yards in less than 5 seconds), is the time it takes the "average shooter" to recognize the threat, draw, aim, and shoot the threat.

Note: The potential distance an average man can travel and function after receiving a fatal wound is 210 feet/70 yards in 14 seconds.

Jeopardy

Ability and opportunity do not complete the reasonable apprehension of a deadly threat. The threat must also demonstrate a willful intent to carry out an attack and you must fear that your life is in jeopardy. For instance, if your co-worker, within arms reach (WAR) from you, is testing the edge of a new switchblade at a gun show, he has both ability and opportunity—but you do not have the reasonable perception that he is intent on hurting you, and you do not feel that your life is in jeopardy.

Ability, opportunity, and *jeopardy* form a tripod often referred to as "the totality of the circumstances." If all three are not present simultaneously, you cannot prove justifiable use of force.

Neutralize the Threat

Surviving a deadly encounter is always your No. 1 priority. In light of that, as the great Col. Jeff Cooper once said, "Where to aim is fully as important as how to aim." He was right. When we shoot a threat it is solely to neutralize him in self-defense. We do not shoot to maim, we do not fire warning shots, we simply shoot at threats to neutralize them.

In most situations we train to shoot at center-mass. The chest is the easiest and quickest to hit and contains the heart, lungs, and many large blood-filled organs and vessels.

An effective shot will essentially cause a person's nervous system to shut down. Less than a second or so after the first round hits, the nervous systems begins an involuntary protective shutdown process.

Given the extremely short duration within which the shutdown process occurs, you will generally have time for two to three shots. If the center-mass shots fail to neutralize the threat, consider a good head shot, specifically the cranio-ocular (brain/eyes) cavity.

There are some reports circulating that indicate only a small percentage of shooters have the ability to make effective head shots. But the most recent data on handgun confrontations has shown that the average pistol confrontation takes place at less than three meters and that a good head shot is possible for the majority of shooters.

The pelvic shot is typically taught to stop a rushing attacker armed with an edged or blunt weapon. If the pelvic girdle is struck, the threat generally does crumble; however he is not in any way prevented from continuing the fight from the ground. Most forensic pathologists will tell you, if he's struck in the head area with a good shot, he will be neutralized.

As mentioned above, law enforcement studies indicate multiple threats are on the rise and the shooter's tactics and procedures must be effective in reacting to multiple threats. Instead of shooting one threat until it is neutralized, consider shooting each threat quickly—but only once—and then swing from your strong to weak side hitting the other threats. Continue reassessing the situation and re-engage any other threats. If you have the time, consider shooting the closest or the threat you consider to be the most dangerous first.

LIVING IN A BATTLEFIELD

Lieutenant Colonel David Grossman, an internationally recognized scholar, author, speaker, and one of the world's leading experts in the field of human aggression and the roots of violence and violent crime, is probably best known for his groundbreaking book *On Killing*, which was nominated for a Pulitzer Prize. Grossman was also a professor of psychology at West Point and an Army Ranger during his 23 years in the military.

Most anyone alive could spend years studying the roots of the violence permeating our everyday world and never approach Grossman's expertise on the subject. I have learned a great deal from this brilliant man and have taught his philosophy principles for many years. You'll see his findings extensively sourced and quoted in the Combat Mindset chapter of this text. This is a privilege Grossman not only allows but encourages. Of course, this being only a small portion of his overall research, I'd encourage anyone interested in finding out more to try and see Grossman speak, order his books and DVDs, or at least visit his Web site, www.killology.com, where he has compiled a broad range of his writings and thoughts on the subject. I have never found anyone with a better handle on why human beings are so violent or the roots of the battlefield in which we walk the streets and raise our children.

In a groundbreaking article Grossman wrote for *Christianity Today* titled "Killology," he stated that to understand the causes of the outbreak of violence in America, we need to first come to grips with the magnitude of the problem. It's immense. The per-capita murder rate doubled in the United States between 1957—when the FBI started keeping track of the data—and 1992. An even more startling picture is painted by the rate at which human beings are attempting to kill one another—the aggravated assault rate. That rate in America has gone up from around 60 per 100,000 in 1957 to more than 440 per 100,000 by the mid-1990s. As bad as this is, it would be much worse were it not for two major factors.

> "Act in the valley so that you need not fear those who stand on the hill."
> —Danish Proverb

"First," Grossman writes, "is the increase in the rate at which violent offenders are sent to prison: The prison population in America nearly quadrupled between 1975 and 1992. According to criminologist John J. DiIulio, 'Dozens of credible empirical analyses . . . leave no doubt that the increased use of prisons averted millions of serious crimes.' If not for our tremendous imprisonment rate (the highest of any industrialized nation in the world), the aggravated assault rate and the murder rate would undoubtedly be even higher."

"Second," Grossman continues, in a more unexpected correlation, "the murder rate would be much worse if it weren't for new medical technology. According to the U.S. Army Medical Service Corps, a wound that would have killed you nine-out-of-ten times in World War II, you would have survived nine-out-of-ten times in Vietnam. What this means to us is that it is a very conservative statement to say that, if we had a 1940-level medical technology today, the murder level would be 10 times higher than it is. The magnitude of the problem has been held down by the development of ever more sophisticated life saving skills and techniques, such as helicopter medevacs, 911 operators, paramedics, CPR, and trauma centers."

There is no single reason why our crime rate has grown so disgustingly high. Yes, there are far too many guns floating through society in hands they don't belong; but as Grossman aptly points out, the increase in violence exists on a global scale, even in countries where it's extraordinarily difficult to obtain a gun, and where you can be punished severely if found with one. So why has violence gotten so out of control?

The answer, he writes, lies in the fact that "only one new variable is present in every single one of these countries, and that is violence in the media being presented as entertainment for children."

Grossman calls this phenomenon "killing unnaturally," a conclusion he gleaned from his years spent learning how to "enable people to kill," as he puts it. "Believe me, we are very good at it. It doesn't come naturally—you have to be taught to kill. And just as the military enables killing, we are indiscriminately doing the same thing to our kids, but without the safeguards."

Human beings, including children, learn to kill through "abuse and violence in the home and, most pervasively, from violence as entertainment in television, the movies and interactive video games," Grossman writes. It makes sense if you think about it. How easy is it to push the "shoot" button on a Nintendo, PlayStation or Xbox controller? Yet when that happens, and the man on the screen is shot dead, there is no recourse for a child to relate to. The dead man's family doesn't grieve. You don't see his parents or wife or children crying. Likewise, nobody comes to take the child who pushed the button off to jail. If anything, he may be praised by his friend or brother for achieving a desired result on the television or computer screen.

In real life everything is different. "When human beings are overwhelmed with anger and fear," left pondering what drastic measures to take next, Grossman writes, "we slam head-on into resistance in the forebrain that generally prevents us from killing. Every healthy human being—with the exception of sociopaths, who by definition don't have that resistance—has this innate violence immune system.

"What we observe throughout human history is that when humans fight each other, there always ends up being a lot of posturing. Adversaries make as much loud noise as possible, puffing themselves up, trying to daunt the enemy. There's a lot of fleeing and submission. The ancient battles were nothing more than great shoving matches. It wasn't until one side or the other turned and ran that the vast majority of killing happened, and most of that involved one person stabbing another in the back."

Over time, as human beings evolved, their inclination to kill changed—but only slightly. You often hear people talk about something being "in a person's DNA." If ever there were a question as to whether the killing instinct fit that bill, a World War II soldier's enterprising inquisition helped to dispel it.

He was U.S. Army Brigadier General S. L. A. Marshall, and during the war he directed a team of researchers to study something that hadn't previously been explored in such a fashion. Marshall's idea was basic, but also as revolutionary as it was fascinating. "Soldiers were asked to describe what they actually did in battle. What they discovered was that less than 20 percent of the soldiers could actually bring themselves to fire at the enemy."

That was the reality of the battlefield, but times have changed. U.S. military personnel were willing and able to die for their country but the vast majority of the military were not willing to kill or even fire at the enemy. Although this was a phenomenal insight into human nature, the military had a real problem that needed to be corrected. And they did just that.

By the Korean War approximately 55 percent of the soldiers were willing to fire at the enemy and by Vietnam over 90 percent were.

The manners in which our military increased its personnel's will-ingness to kill is startlingly similar to the way our culture is instilling a likemindedness in our children—except our children are obliv-ious to their cooperation. Among the methods the military uses are brutalization, desensitization, classical conditioning, operant condi-tioning, and role modeling.

Brutalization and Desensitization

Brutalization and desensitization occur at law enforcement academies, boot camps, and most other basic level and advanced combat-related courses. Grossman states that trainees' "heads are often shaved, and they are herded together naked and dressed alike, losing all vestiges of individuality. This brutalization is designed to break down your existing norms and force you to accept a new set of values that embrace destruction, violence and"—most significant, in this context—"death as a way of life. In the end you are desensitized to violence and accept it as a normal and essential survival skill in your brutal new world."

In the real world, we see the same kind of phenomenon happening to children. "But instead of 18-year-olds, it begins at the age of 18 months, when a child is first able to discern what's happening on television," Grossman writes. "At that age a child can watch some-thing on television"—say, a law enforcement officer fatally shooting a thug—"and they can mimic that action." The problem? Not until the kids are six or seven years old are they able to distinguish between fantasy and reality.

"This means that when a young child sees somebody being shot, stabbed, raped, brutalized, degraded, or murdered on TV or in a video game, to them it is as though it were actually happening. To have a 4-year-old child watch a 'splatter' movie in which they spend 90 minutes learning to relate to a character and then in the last 30 minutes of the movie watch helplessly as their newfound friend is hunted down and brutally murdered, is the moral and psychological equivalent of introducing your child to a friend, letting them play with that friend, and then butchering that friend in front of your child's eyes right in your living room. And this happens to our children hundreds upon hundreds of times in their young lifetimes."

There are plenty of parents who defend their allowing their kids to watch such grotesque violence on TV or video games by claiming they explain to the kids it's not real. But the true reality is that the kids don't understand the explanation. They have no clue the person they just saw decapitated on TV was never *actually* harmed. It's their innate inability to distinguish real from contrived that can have devastating consequences.

Grossman likes to cite an epidemiological study on the impact of TV violence that appeared in the *Journal of the American Medical Association*. And when you hear the results, it's almost impossible to argue the correlation between violence on screen and violence in real life—a correlation that is now even greater than the proven relationship between cancer and tobacco.

> "The research demonstrated what happened in numerous nations after television made its appearance, as compared to nations and regions without TV and video games. The two nations or regions were designed to be demographically and ethnically identical; only one variable has been manipulated—the presence of television. The findings, once more, proved startling. In every comparison in the overall study, the nation, region, or city where television is introduced shows an immediate explosion of violence on the playground, and within 15 years the murder rate doubles. Why 15 years? That's how long it takes for the young, oblivious brutalization victims to reach the 'prime crime age.'"

We are irresponsible, to say the least, to allow our children to become desensitized through video games, TV programs, and movies that teach and promote killing.

Classical Conditioning

The way the military uses classical conditioning is similar to what is taught in basic psychology—how Pavlov's dog learned to associate the bell's ringing with food. As you may recall, after a spell the dog could not hear the bell without salivating.

In the combat medium, Grossman compares the manner in which the Japanese employed classical conditioning to teach their soldiers to kill without remorse to the way a child might learn to associate killing a foe in a video game with a desirable feeling of accomplishment. "Early in World War II, Chinese prisoners were placed in a ditch on their knees with their hands bound behind them," he writes. "And one by one, young, un-bloodied Japanese soldiers had to go into the ditch and bayonet 'their' prisoner to death. This is a brutal, horrific way to have to kill another human being. Up on the banks there was an officer who would shoot the Japanese soldiers if they did not kill; and all of their friends would cheer them on in their violence. Afterwards, they were treated to the best meal they'd had in months, enough sake to make them feel happy again, and to so-called 'comfort girls.' The result? They learned to associate committing violent acts with pleasure."

> "Minds are like parachutes; they only function when they are open."
> —Sir James Dewar, scientist

In the movie *A Clockwork Orange,* a brutal sociopath and murderer was strapped to a chair and forced to watch violent movies. Unbeknownst to him, a drug was injected into him that made him nauseous and he sat, gagged, and vomited as he watched the movies. After hundreds of repetitions of this he began to associate violence with nausea and it limited his ability to engage in violence.

Grossman states that "what we are doing is the exact opposite of this: we're subjecting our children to vivid pictures of human suffering and death, and they learn to associate it with … what? Their favorite soft drink and candy bar, or their girlfriend's perfume."

One of the most striking anecdotes I've found in Grossman's writings to illustrate the disturbingly soft way in which our kids view violence comes from his experience on the scene of the school shooting in Jonesboro, Arkansas, more than a decade ago.

After the incident, he writes, "One of the high school teachers spoke about her students' reaction when she told them that someone had shot a bunch of their little brothers, sisters and cousins in the middle school. 'They laughed,' she said with dismay. 'They laughed.' A similar reaction happens all the time in movie theaters when there is bloody violence. The young people laugh and cheer and keep right on eating popcorn and drinking soda. We have raised a generation of barbarians who have learned to associate violence with pleasure, like the Romans cheering and snacking as the Christians were slaughtered in the Coliseum.

"The result," he contends, "is a phenomenon which functions much like AIDS and is called *AVIDS*—Acquired Violence Immune Deficiency Syndrome. AIDS has never killed anybody. It destroys your immune system and then other diseases that shouldn't kill you become fatal, like pneumonia for instance. Similarly, television and video game violence itself doesn't kill anybody. It destroys your violence immune system and conditions you to derive pleasure from violence. To kill another human being you've got to get through two filters.

"The first filter is the forebrain; many things can convince the forebrain to kill: racism, politics, religion, anger, temper, greed, hatred, revenge. But once you're at close range with another human being and it's time for you to pull that trigger, you are dealing with forebrain resistance. And that's when AVIDS takes over, allowing people to kill."

Operant Conditioning

The third method the military utilizes to train its personnel to kill is a psychological device known as operant conditioning, a highly effective tool built on a series of stimulus-response repetitions.

The shooting community typically uses realistic, 3-D, "funny-face" or human-shaped targets. That's the conditioned stimulus. The trainees will very quickly have to identify if the target is "threat or non-threat" and are trained to engage only the threats. The conditioned response is to neutralize the threat. The terminology changes from time to time and within different organizations. However, "to stop," "neutralize," or "eliminate the threat" are much more humane ways to say "kill the bad guy."

In stimulus-response training, military and law enforcement officers experience hundreds of repetitions of stimuli and then respond in a certain fashion. Later, when the soldier is engaged in battle or a law enforcement officer faces a threat, reflexively and unconsciously they should all be trained to ID and neutralize the threat. This training works, as sources show that 75–80 percent of all shooting on today's battlefield is the result of this stimulus-response training. Similarly, a well-trained civilian shooter should be trained in the same way since it has been proven time and time again that this method does work.

This training is required for servicemen and women who put their lives on the line in the performance of duty. But every time a child plays an interactive, point-and-shoot video game, he's unintentionally learning the exact same conditioned reflex and motor skills the military teaches.

"One of the two children involved in the Jonesboro shootings (11 and 13 years old) allegedly had a fair amount of experience shooting real guns," Grossman writes. "The other child was a non-shooter and, to the best of our knowledge, had almost no experience shooting. Those two kids between them fired 27 shots from a range of over 100 yards, and they hit 15 people. That's pretty remarkable accuracy. We run into these situations a lot: kids who have never picked up a gun in their lives suddenly grab a real weapon and are astonishingly accurate and efficient with that gun, thanks to today's video games."

Role Models

Another teaching tool the military, and to some degree the law enforcement community, uses to teach to kill is the influence and use of the "role model." Military personnel are surrounded by role models: drill sergeants, BUD/s (Basic Underwater Demolition/SEALs) instructors, war heroes, et al. These folks generally represent authority, demand respect, and reinforce the use of controlled violence and aggressiveness—powerful, effective, and necessary tools used to train those going into harm's way on a regular basis.

Likewise, Grossman points out, "today the media are providing our children with role models. But it's not just the crazy sociopaths in movies and TV shows." The phenomenon is also witnessed in the number of media-inspired, copycat killings such as Jonesboro, Columbine, and Virginia Tech, a twist to these juvenile crimes that the media would rather not report.

"Research, back in the early '70s, demonstrated the effect of 'cluster suicides,' in which the local TV reporting of teen suicides was said to be directly responsible for numerous copycat suicides committed by other young teenagers."

Because of this research, media today generally do not cover suicides. But when the pictures of teenage killers appear in the media, the effect is essentially the same; somewhere there is a potentially violent little boy who says to himself, "I'll show all those people who have been mean to me. I know how to get my picture in the news too."

This effect, Grossman argues, materializes like a virus spread by 24-hour news reporting. No matter what someone has done, if their picture appears on TV and Web sites, you have made them a celebrity, and someone will want to emulate them.

"It's vital that our society be informed of these crimes," he writes, "but when the visual images of the young killers are put in the media, they have just become role models." According to TV-Free America, the average child watches TV 1,680 minutes per week vs. 3.5 minutes per week in which parents spend in meaningful conversation with their children. Even 70 percent of day care centers report using TV throughout the day. The number of murders seen on TV by the time an average child finishes elementary school is 8,000, and the number of violent acts seen on TV by age 18 is a staggering 200,000. When adding in the amount of time a child spends playing video games, the situation is much worse.

Gun Control

One definition of gun control is "to be able to effectively hit what you are trying to hit." Another definition may be "you can achieve gun control through proper stance, proper sight alignments, proper grip and trigger control; applied repeatedly until the threat is neutralized." These definitions are true, but there is another definition that is also relevant to this text.

As I sit and put the final touches on this book while deployed overseas, a co-worker was just shot in the neck. It was a through-and-through shot and miraculously he is expected to recover from this wound with only minimal complications. The threat just happened to get a lucky hit on him.

Those on the political left as well as those on the right of this issue must face the fact that humans have always and will always possess weapons. Some may think we can ban them from everybody—but that is idealistic and would be impossible. I do not want to live in a place where law-abiding citizens are not armed and the outlaws are.

The words "gun control" conjure terrible images for most of us who own weapons. In the early 1990s I was asked to be a delegate for presidential candidate Senator Bob Kerry, a Vietnam war hero, SEAL, and Medal of Honor recipient. I initially turned down this honor since he was an advocate of gun control. It is difficult to find military personnel or military supporters who are pro gun control.

Richard Kostner, who was trying to recruit me for this position and was very much active in presidential politics, told me that I would never have a problem owning a weapon nor would my law-abiding friends and families have a problem owning a weapon under Senator Kerry's proposed legislation on gun control. The only people who would not be entitled to own a gun would be the criminals and those who could not pass the background checks. I wish it were that simple.

> "Laws that forbid the carrying of arms . . . disarm only those who are neither inclined nor determined to commit crimes . . . Such laws make things worse for the assaulted and better for assailants; they serve rather to encourage than to prevent murders."
> —Thomas Jefferson

My 21-year-old stepson, Christian, was just getting ready to graduate college with honors. Two weeks prior to graduation Christian was shot and murdered by two gang members. In many states, murderers like these and other criminals are able to walk into gun shows, swap meets, pawn shops, and sporting stores and purchase weapons themselves. These thugs acquire weapons not for hunting, home defense, military, law enforcement, or competition, but so they can shoot people at will. My strong personal feeling on gun control is that we need to do our best to prevent people like these from owning guns and penalize them severely if they are caught possessing them.

However, to deny a nation of citizens the right to own guns is a dangerous prospect. History tells us that. According to a widely distributed anti-gun control message, in the twentieth century some 56 million citizens were exterminated from their homelands by oppressive governments in the wake of "gun control laws" being imposed. This trend spanned the planet, including the former Soviet Union, China, Cambodia, Guatemala, and Uganda, among others. In Australia, the recent passing of gun control laws preceded a stunning spike in violent crimes, which many have attributed to the fact that criminals no longer must worry that their law-abiding victims are armed.

In America, everyone remembers or has heard of the Japanese air raid on Pearl Harbor in December 1941. One lesser-known fact that was reported in the wake of that devastation is that the Japanese didn't feel comfortable following up that attack with an invasion on American soil because the Japanese Admiral Yamamoto—who masterminded the Pearl Harbor raid—had attended college in the States and knew that a great percentage of our citizens bore arms.

Americans, then, are caught in a vicious cycle when it comes to gun control. Many gun owners own guns simply because they do not have faith in our government. This I understand! Law-abiding American citizens should always have the right and responsibility for taking care of and protecting themselves and their families.

So weapons are purchased and used for home and workplace defense, personal protection, and for recreation. Unfortunately, the fact remains that while more weapons often mean less violence, there are also some instances where they mean more violence. And the more violence, the greater our defensive need for weapons. It is among the most vicious circles.

This chain of events is our reality. For many of us, the only way we will ever feel secure and protected is to be able to protect ourselves with a weapon when and if required. Life, indeed, is a battlefield.

"A strong body makes the mind strong. As to the species of exercises, I advise the gun. While this gives moderate exercise to the body, it gives boldness, enterprise, and independence to the mind . . . Let your gun therefore be the constant companion of your walks."

—Thomas Jefferson

COMBAT MINDSET

"Never interrupt your enemy when he is making a mistake."
—Napoleon Bonaparte

In the world of gunslinging, building defensive weapons skills is like building a pyramid that we will never complete, because we will never totally master the skills. The first brick, the foundation, is combat mind-set. If we do not lay this brick first, the rest of the training will be a waste of time.

A mind-set is traditionally defined as an established way of thinking. We all have our own mind-set. But certain theorists—notable among them, Stanford University psychology professor Carol Dweck—have

Training Tip: Action is always quicker than reaction: the average time for a person's neurological system to respond to a known stimuli or indicator is a quarter of a second. We will typically react at least a second behind the assailant. A threat that is already acting against you has already gone through the neurological process and you have not, therefore you are already at a disadvantage. If you are not prepared for a threat, your neurological response time will be longer.

since argued not every mind-set is so fixed. A growth mind-set, for example, is one in which you see yourself as fluid, a work in progress. In this text, I hope to point out how to develop your life's mind-set into a *combat mind-set*.

> **Training Tip:** In most shooting situations you will be behind the curve. You must be aware of your environment and always expect the unexpected. The assailant will pick the time and place of the gunfight.

The most important factor in a life-or-death encounter will always be your combat mind-set, which includes, among other things, your fighting spirit, killer instinct, survival instinct, confidence, previous training, past experiences, and will to live.

Every man or woman has a very powerful weapon—the mind. Weapons are just tools; it is our mind that controls how we will use our tools.

Survival Awareness

Our ancestors had to survive in a world that was wild, unpredictable, and dangerous. Similarly, in these modern times we too have to survive in a world that is wild, unpredictable, and in many ways even more dangerous than times before.

Since I have been traveling to war zones and places of "unrest" for the past thirty years or so, I have no choice but to continually maintain, sharpen, and fine-tune my own combat mind-set, my "survivor's awareness." I see no reason to turn this off once I get back stateside because, as we all know, we have threats roaming throughout our country and these threats only seem to multiply year after year. I am not paranoid, just aware of my own surroundings and confident of my training and ability to react to emerging threats.

You may be one of the best shots in the world, but if you don't see the attack coming, all of your fine skills can be of little or no value. I am not suggesting you become fearful, just stay alert.

If you carry a weapon it only makes sense that you are able to operate and fire your weapon competently (hopefully in the unconscious competent phase, which will be discussed later). If you have to stop and think about your actions, you may be seconds too slow to survive a confrontation.

Combat Mindset

Combat mind-set is the most important part of the shooter's triangle. The marksmanship skills and tactics involved with shooting will be useless if you don't possess the proper combat mind-set. The good news is that developing a combat mind-set—unlike marksmanship training and tactics training—can be practiced and strengthened each and every day. With the right mind-set, you can survive a confrontation even without the benefit of recent time on the range or practicing tactics.

Anticipation Mindset

A critical element of combat mind-set is "anticipation mindset." By practicing anticipation mind-set, you are simply solving problems before actually confronting them. Visualize what might happen, then prepare yourself to take action.

If you hear a noise in your basement, you wouldn't go into the basement not expecting to see anything. You would anticipate that somebody may have broken into your home and you would be ready to deal with the threat. If you have noticed that a vehicle has made every turn you have and ended up following you home, you should anticipate that it may be more than just mere coincidence. Maybe you're being followed because the person wants to hurt, rob, kidnap, or kill you.

You make yourself ready, have a plan, and try not to be the one who gets surprised. When a SWAT team member or a SEAL kicks down a door, he is anticipating a battle and is ready to fight. You can apply the same philosophy to your own combat mind-set.

Anticipation is a sign of dili-
gence—the mastery of discipline
over oneself. There are two types of
anticipation: planned and response.
Both are critical to performance.
For example, professional athletes,

> **Training Tip:** Stay in
> the fight until the fight is
> over and do whatever it
> takes to win. Never quit.

trainers, and coaches think *strategically* and *tactically* about their plan
to succeed before a game or an event. They analyze their opponent as
well as themselves, and come up with a plan to achieve victory. But at
some point during their performance, the planning becomes irrelevant
unless there's also an ability to adapt the plan to the actual situation,
thereby *responding* to changes in conditions, environment, etc. This is
the demonstration of *operational* thinking and remaining flexible.

To be able to react to any threat, you need a plan and you need
to have the ability to modify the plan quickly. In the SEAL teams,
remaining "flexible" was a characteristic all operators required. "War
is chaos," but with proper planning and the ability to remain flexible,
it can become "controlled chaos."

You may have the best weapon and ammunition available, and
you may have spent countless hours on the range fine-tuning your
marksmanship skills. Your tactics are well-rehearsed, your family and
co-workers know the plan, and when the threat emerges, you will
shoot, move, communicate, and take cover in accordance with the
plan. Your tactics will be up against the ultimate test. But all of that
is not enough if you are unaware of your surroundings and don't see
the threat coming.

All of that said, if the threat gets a jump on you and catches you
unprepared, stay in the fight. You haven't lost and you will not lose—
that's the essence of the combat mind-set. Yes, you may get wounded,
but you will do whatever it takes to stay in the fight, because you have
to win. There are simply no other options.

This is where Cooper's color code is of such value, as discussed
later in this chapter. By the time you reach "condition red," which

Training Tip: In most shooting situations you will be behind the curve. Reaction time will not be at action time. You must be aware of your environment and always expect the unexpected.

means you're protecting your life, you no longer have to worry about anything else but acting out your plan to fight or flee.

Mental awareness, a key element to combat mind-set, is enhanced when utilizing your anticipation mind-set. An important part of mental awareness is learning to listen to your gut feelings, which are an accumulation of your experiences and training. If you notice a group of gangbangers clustered near the entrance of a liquor store in your path, change your path. Avoid a confrontation whenever possible. Do not make yourself available to the threat, but have a plan and be ready to react if need be. The best way to win a fight is to steer clear of it. Barring that, the next best thing is to know that it is coming and to make the threat fight and lose on your terms.

If your mind has not been trained or conditioned, if you haven't developed a combat mind-set, the threat can beat you with nothing more than his own will, attitude, and mind-set.

Fight or Flight Response

One of the primary elements in a combat mind-set comes from the "fight or flight response," our body's natural instinct to react to a perceived threat.

When we experience excessive stress, a bodily reaction is triggered. Harvard physiologist Walter Cannon explains that this response can be traced to an area of our brain called the hypothalamus, which, when stimulated by fear or stress, initiates a sequence of nerve cell firing and chemical release that prepares our body to fight or flee.

There are physiological signs and symptoms you will experience when in the fight-or-flight mode. Every person experiences these signs and symptoms differently. It is important that you know how you will react when you are faced with a life and death situation. The physical reactions include muscle tension, headache, upset stomach, tunnel vision, increased heartbeat, shallow breathing, anxiety, poor concentration, hopelessness, frustration, anger, sadness, fear, and/or auditory occlusion.

Although fight or flight is every animal's response to a threat, humans are highly intelligent animals and can overcome the natural urge to flee, and wade into a fight instead. Most of us are civilized beings and not psychotic, cold-blooded killers. But we still must be able to apply the appropriate degree of force when necessary, and we must be able to kill with ruthless efficiency if need be.

Regardless of whether you find yourself in fight or flight mode, you have to remain in control. Do not panic. Through training based-scenarios you will learn your own strengths, weaknesses, and vulnerabilities. You will also find that if you can stay in control and remain calm and collected it can generate a calming effect on those around you. And this can make a world of difference.

Again, I am not suggesting that we all need to live in a world of paranoia or the expectation that something terrible is about to happen. But I am suggesting that you develop a sense confidence by having the knowledge, skills, and attitude that you will prevail when or if you are confronted by a threat.

Visualization

Through visualization many athletes develop a thought process that reduces stress, increases confidence, improves self-awareness and control, and leads to better form, quicker improvements, and enhanced performance. As a shooter you can also benefit in similar ways.

Visualization during Training

Picture yourself firing off a number of precise, tightly grouped, center-mass shots in rapid succession. This will allow you to fragment the shooting process into the different fundamentals that allow such precision: stance, grip, trigger control, sight alignment, and follow-through.

By focusing on each subset individually, you're able to break them down to a point where you can actually improve every facet of your shooting, which then enables better overall performance, be it on the range or in an actual life or death situation.

Visualization requires self-discipline as well as a discerning eye for which aspects of shooting you want to refine. It is important to self-analyze your own shooting, step by step. A tip that many professionals share is to begin working on the specific skill or movement that you feel is your weakest, the one needing the most improvement. Once you have that movement perfected, move to your next skill or movement needing improvement. This is a never-ending process because no matter how much you train, you will never reach true perfection but you will always be able to work at getting more accurate, smoother, faster, and safer. A disciplined shooter will continue to raise the bar. Practice does not make perfect, it is *perfect practice that makes perfect*. The closer you can come to perfection, the better.

Think about breaking down your steps incrementally. For example, you may be able to slow fire a well-placed single shot into the center mass of a target from 15 meters, once your weapon is drawn, but your movement with your strong hand to the holster may not be fluid and/or it may be too slow. You may want to work on acquiring a better grip before "breaking leather," or clearing your weapon from the holster may need some work. Perhaps your pistol movement from the holster to the pivot position—muzzle down position to muzzle-toward-the-target position—may not be efficient. Or perhaps when you bring your weapon up to marry with your support hand may it may be a bit too clumsy. There are literally hundreds of steps you can self-analyze and improve.

A disciplined shooter will analyze every movement, step by step, and will find ways to make that movement smoother, more efficient, and then ultimately quicker. Smooth is fast; the smoother your technique, the faster your technique. It is very helpful to work with another shooter, especially if that person has more experience than you. This is another excellent way to maximize the benefits of dry fire training.

To give you an idea of how well visualization works, Ron Avery, who has long been among the top competitive shooters in the world, once told me that he had to have surgery on his shooting forearm and was left unable to shoot or dry fire for months. But he did visualize every step of every move in his shooting and once he was able to shoot again, he was faster than before his surgery.

Visualization with Tactics

Visualization is also very effective in tactics training. Visualize yourself in different scenarios; for instance, while driving through a shady part of town, in combat, or when confronted by a threat. If I go into that 7-Eleven and the two suspicious looking characters standing by the door follow me in, what will I do if they hold up the store? Or, let's say the dogs are barking, but when you look out the window you do not see anything. Then you hear a noise in the kitchen. Visualize what you would do and when it happens for real it is that much easier and less traumatic to take action. Perhaps all you would do is lock the door, gather those in your home into one room, call 911, stay quiet, and be ready to protect your loved ones with however many shots it may take. Having all of this thought out beforehand makes the actual situation all the more controlled.

If attacked, I will be prepared and will know what to do. I routinely practice visualization and go over scenarios in my mind: *If this happens, I will do this . . . If that happens, I will do that.* It's not an inconvenience, it just makes sense. For me, it makes the same sense as driving a car with working brakes. And it's a good feeling to know I'm ready if and when the threat appears. People don't plan or hope to be in a car accident, but it gives them peace of mind to have auto insurance. It's the same way with being prepared for an attack.

When traveling, my plans include utilizing visualization techniques. Whether in the Middle East, Central or South America, or the former Soviet Bloc countries, I have a plan. For instance, I know that if my room is broken into, I will, most likely, have my M4 or AK placed on a towel, on the floor next to my bed, pointed toward the door. The weapon will have a full magazine in it and will be on safe. Next to the weapon are my radio, cell phone, flashlight, and Glock with a 15-round magazine.

When driving overseas, I will ask my partner to also stay alert, to keep a careful eye through the windshield, the passenger mirror, and the right side of the vehicle. He is to verbalize anything that looks suspicious.

We can go on in life thinking that terrorists and criminals only attack other people. Or, we can accept the reality that attacks happen often and to people of all walks of life and to people all over the world. It is a dangerous world and it is very naive to think an attack can not happen to you.

It is important to always visualize success in whatever situations you're visualizing; otherwise this type of training can have an adverse effect on what it is intended to accomplish.

Sheep, Wolves, and Sheepdogs

The vast majority of Americans are not inclined to hurt one another, but over two million U.S. citizens are victims of violent crimes every year. There are almost 300 million of us, so the odds of being a victim of violent crime are approaching one in a hundred during any given year.

It is hard to believe so many human beings can be grouped into just three categories, but in this context it works really well. First are the wolves. They're the evil men and women, the "threat" living among the rest of us. They're unpredictable and, in many cases, deadly. Grossman describes wolves as aggressive sociopaths "who will feed on the flock without mercy." He continues, "The moment

Left: David Grossman, creator of the sheep, wolves, and sheepdogs analogy giving a very motivating talk to a group of police officers and security professionals. Below: David Grossman signing autographs after giving another very motivating talk to a group of police officers and security professionals.

you forget that or pretend it is not so, you become a sheep. There is no safety in denial."

Sheep, then, are the harmless human beings who live among the wolves and are always in jeopardy of becoming prey. "If you are a healthy productive citizen with no proclivity toward violence," Grossman writes, "then you are a sheep." Sheep are trusting, often too much so. That's why they are perennially in danger. The woman who walks through a dimly lit parking lot at 2 AM with no hesitation as a strange man approaches is a sheep, and maybe the wolf's dinner.

However, there are also those who possess a protective side, as well as a love and respect for their fellow human beings. These are the sheepdogs that live among us. They are the good guys; they are you and I. Grossman calls a sheepdog "a warrior who is walking the hero's path, one who walks into the heart of darkness, and emerges unscathed." All of those in the military ("the sword") and in law enforcement ("the shield") are our fellow sheepdogs.

Most of the people in our society are sheep, Grossman contends. They are kind, gentle, productive creatures who can only hurt one another by accident. And this is true. The vast majority of Americans, and for that matter, people of any nation, are not inclined to inflict harm on another.

"The sheep," Grossman writes, "generally do not like the sheepdog. He looks like the wolf. He has fangs and the capacity for violence. The difference, though, is that the sheepdog must not, cannot, and will not, ever purposely harm the sheep. But the sheepdog does disturb the sheep. He is a constant reminder that there are wolves in the land. They would prefer that the sheepdog didn't give the sheep traffic tickets, stand at the ready in our airports in camouflage fatigues carrying M4s, or go off to wars and be proactive against the wolves. The sheep would much rather have the sheepdog turn in his fangs and just believe that violence will simply disappear."

We are always going to have a mix of wolves, sheep, and sheepdogs in society. Some people, as Grossman puts it, "were destined to be sheep and others might be genetically primed to be wolves or sheepdogs. But, most people can choose which one they want to be, and in this chaotic world, more and more Americans are choosing to become sheepdogs."

Cooper's Colors

After the events of 9/11, our country began to learn about a color-coded advisory system created by the Department of Homeland Security to depict the current threat of terrorist activity. This system is not all that different from the awareness color code developed by Colonel Jeff Cooper, one of the founding fathers of the International Practical Shooting Confederation (IPSC). Cooper's color code consists of levels of perceived danger, each represented by a color—white, yellow, orange, and red, in order of awareness and increasing danger. (Black was added years later.)

As the level of perceived danger increases, your resistance to use deadly force decreases. If you ever end up in condition red, the decision to use lethal force should have already been made. In this condition you are no longer worried about your career, family, etc . . . It is simply a matter of life and death.

Below is a brief description of the Cooper Color Code related through the experience of driving, a tactic utilized by well-known law enforcement instructor C. Allen Reed in the context of self-defense.

Condition White:

According to Reed, someone living in condition white isn't ready to face life's inherent dangers. "Remember the last time you blew through an intersection and then realized there had been a stop sign?" he wrote. "Or the last time you were stopped at a red light and the driver behind you had to beep his horn to remind you the light had changed to green? Both of these times you were in *white*. You were day-dreaming or thinking of something else instead of being focused on what was going on around you. This happens all the time."

Think about the times that someone you know has passed you in the hall and you weren't aware of their being there until they were right on top of you. You were in condition white. Most people spend much of their lives in condition white, which is why so many crime victims claim they never saw their attacker until the attack had begun.

In Cooper's code, condition white represents a lack of awareness. Being in condition white while in the presence of the wolf can get you killed quickly and easily. The wolf looks for those in condition white. When traveling in or living in terrorist- or criminal-rich environments, going to condition white is not an option.

Sheep typically live their days in condition white because they refuse to accept the fact that the wolf may be planning an attack on them, because the wolf only attacks "other people." It is easier to live in condition white, which is why so many people do.

Thus the person in condition white has built a barrier to the use of deadly force—denial. If you are attacked in white, you will most likely lose the fight. You may not even notice there was a fight—the lights will simply go out.

Condition Yellow:

Living in condition yellow entails an enhanced state of skepticism about everything you see and hear around you. "You are looking in the rearview mirror for that rapidly approaching car weaving in and out of traffic. You are looking ahead to see the lights of the law enforcement car off on one side of the road. You are looking for someone who may be hiding in the shadows near the entrance to your apartment building," Reed explained. Condition yellow is a manner of relaxed awareness.

When a man is in condition yellow he is aware that *today may be the day.* He is not in a combat mode, nor is he aware of any specific situation that may call for action on his part.

If you are attacked in condition white, you will probably die, or at least need medical care; if you are attacked in condition yellow, you have a better chance of defeating the threat.

The difference does not lie in the deadliness of the hazard facing you, but rather in your willingness to remain alert and take proactive, life-saving steps before it is too late.

My wife has her own set of tactics for home defense. If I am not home, and someone gets into our house in the middle of the night, she knows and has practiced exactly what to do. She will ramp up from white to yellow to red, in a heartbeat if need be.

She is armed and is comfortable with her tactics. The only thing we have not covered in our home tactics is who will clean the rug and the walls once the threat has been neutralized. Any time we go out to a restaurant, we both know that I will have my back to the wall, and generally we both remain in condition yellow.

In yellow, you will have the advantage of initiative response over the threat.

Condition Orange:

In this state of *heightened awareness*, Reed claimed, "Something has alerted you to a possible problem and you are prepared to make a decision and act on it. Examples include: The ball bouncing out into the street from between parked cars; the car that seems to be going just a bit too fast at the intersection up ahead, as if the driver has not seen the stop sign on his side of the intersection; or the guy loitering near your car in the parking lot for no apparent reason. These are all possible problems that you may need to solve very quickly."

If, in the course of events, you become aware of the possible existence of a possible threat in your presence, you switch to condition orange. If you were in yellow, you would say to yourself, "I may have to shoot today. I may actually have to press my trigger on a human adversary, but I don't know who or where." When you detect the presence of a threat who could be the one you will have to engage, you shift from yellow to orange.

Someone in condition orange has recognized a potential threat, and the barrier has dropped. In condition red the specific threat has been identified and the barrier has been removed. The threat's further behavior will determine whether the defender needs to employ deadly force. In orange, you are fairly safe, provided you are armed.

Colonel Jeff Cooper put it this way: "In *Condition Orange*, the mind-set is—I may have to take action to eliminate this threat. At this point, your normal reluctance becomes easier to overcome.

Legal and moral aspects of the conflict are lowered and have been dismissed from your mind. Your attitude is dictated by the presence of that potential threat standing there. *You may have to shoot him now—any second.* What is needed is a trigger. The trigger is the act that establishes the situation as a matter of lethal conflict."

Condition Red:

It's time to act. "In this state," Reed wrote, "the bouncing ball *was* followed by the kid; the other driver *did* fail to stop at the stop sign; the guy loitering by your car is now rapidly approaching you. In other words, the crisis has arrived, and if you do not make the right decision and make it *right now,* someone could be seriously hurt or killed."

In condition red you know judgment day has arrived. You're concerned with one thing and one thing only: neutralizing the threat.

Once you recognize that someone is a threat, you can't afford to remain in a purely reactive mode. If you merely react to the threat, you will remain behind the power curve since action is always faster than reaction. You must gain the initiative and force the threat to react to your moves.

In condition red, you win. You cannot go any further than red because in red you have already made the lethal decision.

One of the greatest and most widely known gunslingers of the Wild West was James Butler "Wild Bill" Hickok. Wild Bill was a scout for the Union army during the Civil War, and gained fame as a frontier marshal and gunfighter in Kansas. He also toured with Buffalo Bill demonstrating his legendary shooting abilities to audiences around the country. On Aug. 2, 1876, while he was playing poker in a saloon in Deadwood, South Dakota, Wild Bill was shot from behind and killed by Jack McCall. If this legendary shooter had been in condition orange and then red, he would have been alert enough to prevent his untimely death.

People do let their guards down and it is impossible to always be in orange, because it will burn you out. The solution is to know when to switch conditions. Too often people have lost their lives because they either get too confident or become too trusting in the vicinity of the wolf.

Condition Black:

Condition black is simply the condition people tend to go to from condition white when attacked. Cooper did not include this in his original color code, but we have all seen people in condition black. It may be the person driving while talking on a cell phone, listening to music and not paying attention—then just after this person comes around a curve and comes face-to-face with a large tractor-trailer truck in his lane, he freezes. He was not aware of his surroundings and did not anticipate that another vehicle would do this. He did not use his senses nor was he alert to his surroundings. He lost his life.

Another example: As you read this text, your door is suddenly kicked in and three masked gunmen are holding you and your family at gunpoint. You did not see or hear this coming and you freeze. Always avoid going into condition black.

In summary, moving among the various conditions is easy to accomplish once the code is understood. The color code of preparedness exists to encourage people to be aware that the need to employ deadly force may occur in their everyday lives. Always be prepared. Don't underestimate your need to be prepared. Don't make it easy for the wolf.

Situational Awareness

Avoid the threat whenever possible and be able to recognize the threat. More than 85 percent of civilian defense cases involve people we know; however, people tend to fear the unknown more than they fear those who are close to us.

The more you know your environment and plan appropriate defensive responses through anticipation mind-set and visualization, the more aware and safer you become.

The threat can appear anywhere and at anytime, and this I will never forget. When traveling to a wolf's den, it only makes sense to be extra vigilant. During those times, my senses will often warn me and help dictate my course of action.

It is imperative to have well-thought-out decisions made in advance so that when confronted by a threat, your decisions are sound. A saying we used in the SEAL teams was to "plan your dive and to dive your plan."

Colonel Boyd's OODA Loop

Colonel Boyd's OODA Loop is another widely accepted awareness tactic used throughout the shooting community.

Observation:

The highest priority. Put simply, this means to find the threat before it finds you. Do not let yourself be surprised by a threat. This is easier said than done, but it is worth striving for.

Many people try to observe their immediate surroundings, but often neglect the far (two buildings away, the tinted sedan four cars behind you), the high (the upper windows, the roof tops, mountain tops), and the low (under furniture, behind vehicles, etc).

Orientation:

After you've had a chance to look around and see what your situation holds, orient yourself to those surroundings and the scenario as a whole. And at the same time do all you can to disorient your threat. Use

Quick tip: When walking down a city street, use the reflection of the windows to aid in your observation.

distance, obstacles (parked cars, buildings, etc.), and angles (those that will boost your chances) to your advantage. Don't make decisions that might be easy for your adversary to predict. Think a step ahead.

Decision:

The subconscious and conscious mind processes hundreds of variables simultaneously to evaluate a potentially threatening situation. The conscious mind will offer the action with the highest probability of success, based on your previous training, experiences, etc. All of the time you spent on the range practicing your pursuit of perfection through repetition will eventually transfer your skill sets from your conscious mind to your subconscious mind. Once these skills are set in the subconscious mind, you will not have to actively decide what tactic to perform, it will instinctively occur. But this will only happen through repetition.

There are varying theories on just how many repetitions are required to entrench a skill or tactic in the subconscious mind, but the majority of trainers feel it is between 1,500 and 3,000 reps.

Action:

Right or wrong, this is the phase where most of your time in training has been spent. *Fight or flight?* You've prepared yourself. You avoid walking by the shady characters, de-escalate the situation, call for help, shoot, communicate, take cover. *Act* on your plan. If the threat does *x,* then you will do *y.* Do not get caught without a plan. A poor plan vigorously executed is better than no plan at all.

If you are hurt, that is okay, because once the threat is neutralized you will receive medical care and you will survive. You must believe this. This has to be part of your mind-set. And you must not worry about surviving while in the fight, because it will distract you. You must believe that you will win any confrontation.

There are thousands of stories of civilians, soldiers, Marines, SEALs, law enforcement officers, and others who have been wounded, many times with multiple wounds, and they went on to win the fight. Convince yourself that if wounded, you will survive, and you will stay in the fight until the threat is eliminated. Don't underestimate the power of this belief.

There is an old saying often printed on T-shirts worn by SEALs that reads, "Break glass in case of war." I always liked to see this because it reminds me that although the SEAL may be out having fun with his buddies, if all hell suddenly broke loose, the glass would be shattered and the warrior would appear. I think all gunslingers should adopt this same attitude.

Shooting Maxims

"The purpose of fighting is to win. There is no possible victory in defense. The sword is more important than the shield and skill is more important than either. The final weapon is the brain, and all else is supplemental."

—John Steinbeck

"There is only one tactical principle which is not subject to change. It is to use the means at hand to inflict the maximum amount of wound, death, and destruction on the enemy in the minimum amount of time."

—General George S. Patton

"A warrior must remember who/what he represents . . . always."

—Anonymous

"If you find yourself in a fair fight, you failed to properly plan beforehand."

—Anonymous

"It is fatal to enter into war without the will to win."

—General Douglas MacArthur, 1952

"If you know the enemy and know yourself, you need not fear the result of a hundred battles. If you know yourself but not the enemy, for every victory gained you will suffer a defeat. If you know neither the enemy, nor yourself, you will succumb in every battle."

—Sun Tzu

"There is no safety for honest men except by believing all possible evil of evil men."

—Edmund Burke

"A fully loaded pistol is useless to the man who has an empty magazine between the ears."

—Louis Awerbuck

"Only the dead have seen the end of war."

—Plato

"Never give in. Never, never, never, never! Never yield in any way, great or small, except to convictions of honor and good sense. Never yield to force and the apparently overwhelming might of the enemy . . ."

—Winston Churchill

"Legitimate, personal confidence in one's own ability is the key to victory. Heart rate, blood pressure, and a host of other unavoidable, psychosomatic, bodily reactions are largely irrelevant."

—Ron Avery

"The first attribute of character is the ability to keep your head while all those around you are losing theirs."

—Rudyard Kipling

SHOOTING COMPETENCE

Guns, for the most part, are created to kill. They are used either as offensive or defensive weapons. The military uses them in both modes while law enforcement officers and most civilians use them in the defensive mode. In an ideal world, we wouldn't need weapons of any sort. But we don't live in an ideal world—far from it. So while guns do kill, they also save lives—perhaps even someday your own.

For example, the legendary Marine Corps sniper Carlos Hathcock never felt he was simply just killing the enemy, he felt that he was saving his comrades from being killed by neutralizing those who were killing his fellow servicemen.

Shooting, like any physical discipline, goes through a series of predictable stages. During the early years of weapons training developmental practitioners generally subscribed to the "just do it" approach. One learned by trial and error or by mimicking a skilled shooter. A school of thought was eventually born and the followers of the skilled shooters eventually codified "the way it was done." These guidelines were then used as training guidelines and tactics.

It wasn't long before these training guidelines and tactics underwent a variety of refinement and hyper-refinement processes. This is an ever-evolving process with most disciplines. Unfortunately this process can be problematic and too often while aiming for perfection people end up emphasizing irrelevant points. The end goal can become lost. Data gathering becomes so flawed that the results are doomed either to utter irrelevance, complete uselessness, or both.

In the good old days, gunslingers simply did what worked for them. They relied on instinct and whatever wisdom they could glean from the men who preceded them. This all changed after World War II when analysis and codification processes began in earnest.

The shooting community became somewhat politicized. Weapons and tactics gurus laid down their doctrine and the discipline began making more progress. Thanks to the U.S. military's training programs and lessons learned during World War II, Korea, Vietnam, Panama, Somalia, Grenada, Bosnia, Afghanistan, Iraq, and other conflicts, the craft became more and more refined.

You must train for the situation and the environment. Be careful not to be sucked into training solely based on the constraints of a range, or the whims of convenience of the weapons instructors. When preparing to deploy to Iraq, for example, training needs to be conducted with the Iraqi threat, the Iraqi streets, etc. in mind. If you are training for home defense scenarios, your training should be conducted with the thought that your home may be broken into, you know where your SAFE (safe area for evacuation) area is located, where your weapons are located and how to operate your weapons in the confines of your home.

You must question and analyze your training—is it as effective as it can be? All shooters need basic marksmanship training and refresher training. But you will want to go beyond the basics and train for your specific needs.

"Learning and knowledge are meant to be forgotten, and it is only when this is realized, that you feel perfectly comfortable. The body will move as if automatically, without conscious effort on the part of the swordsman himself. All of the training is there, but the mind is utterly unconscious of it."
—Yagyu Tajima No Kami, Japanese sword master

Conscious Competence Model

A person's competence is his ability to perform a given task. This model is basically a simplified and organized way to explain the stages many go through during their journey to becoming competent in any given discipline—in our case, shooting. This model describes how we go from the "unconscious incompetence" stage to, eventually, the "unconscious competence" stage, where we don't even have to think about the tasks we do—we simply do them when required.

Consider the following information that was developed for the 15th Annual National Tactical Invitational. To understand this concept makes it somewhat simpler for a shooter to organize his shooting micro and macro training goals.

Unconscious Incompetence

The beginning stage is simple. As an *unconscious incompetent,* you are totally unaware of what you do not know. You lack experience, training, knowledge and skills in a certain discipline and are unaware of your deficiency. You can remain in this state indefinitely if you are not trained properly. You are simply not competent in this particular discipline.

Training Tip: You need to train enough so you do not have to think what to do in the time of crisis. It will come instinctively. Train, train and train, and the process will develop.

Unconscious incompetence may put you in one of two positions. Ignorance is bliss, as they say, and you may well be happily naive, not realizing how incompetent you are. Or you may believe you are competent and either do not recognize your incompetence or are covering it up.

Conscious Incompetence

As a *conscious incompetent,* you realize that you are not the expert as you thought you were or thought you could be. The transition to this state from being unconsciously incompetent can be a shocking and sudden realization, for example when you meet others who are clearly more competent than you, or when a friend somehow points

> **Training Tip:** In a fight, your techniques must be reflexive or you probably won't be able to perform them as well under duress, without a great deal of repetitive training.

out your real ability. You can also exist in this state for a long time, depending on how motivated you are to train and learn and the real extent to which you accept your incompetence.

Conscious Competence

Becoming *consciously competent* often takes a while, because learning a new discipline doesn't happen quickly. This process evolves in stages as you learn, forget, plateau, and start again. The more complex the new discipline and the less talent you have for it, the longer it will take to reach conscious competence, and the more frustrated you're likely to become.

Many shooters have reached the conscious competence stage through practicing perfect practice and with a great deal of repetition. These shooters must follow the step-by-step range commands given by a range master, or think out each step while performing the steps in order to be competent. However, most shooters do not progress past this stage or if they do, they revert back quickly.

We must remember—practice does not make perfect, only *perfect* practice makes perfect! Our goal as shooters should be to train to the unconscious competence level and to stay there. And that takes regular, quality perfect practice through repetition.

Unconscious Competence

With proper, effective training the highly motivated and disciplined shooters will reach a point where they no longer have to think about what they are doing. They are competent without the significant effort that characterizes the prior state of conscious competence. Becoming *unconsciously competent* at shooting and tactics takes a great deal of time, motivation and dedication. Being born with great eyesight, hand-eye coordination, and common sense doesn't hurt either.

People who have achieved unconscious competence can perform at a high level without being aware of the precise details of their own behavior. They understand their goals and they recognize whether or not they are achieving their goals. But they are not aware of the specific details of their actions.

In the area of self-defense, the unconsciously competent person knows he or she is responding to a threat and perceives the threat's general response to their own actions. In a gunfight the person defending himself is focused on the threat's aggressive actions and the threat's response to the shots fired by the defender. If the defender is well-trained he will also be scanning the scene for multiple threats and for cover. But if the defender finds cover and decides to move to it, he is probably still focusing on the threat and on fighting all the way to that cover, rather than thinking about how many steps are required to reach safety.

> "Laws that forbid the carrying of arms ... disarm only those who are neither inclined nor determined to commit crimes ... Such laws make things worse for the assaulted and better for the assailants; they serve rather to encourage than to prevent homicides, for an unarmed man may be attacked with greater confidence than an armed man."
> —Thomas Jefferson's *Commonplace Book*, 1774-1776, quoting from *On Crimes and Punishment* by criminologist Cesare Beccaria, 1764

So in this example, the "unconscious" in unconscious competence really refers to how the defender remains focused on the threat, tactics and evolving outcome rather than the precise details of his own behavior.

The term "competence" is context-dependent. A person can be a champion marksman and miss the target completely in a shoot house or in force-on-force training. We see this quite often on the range and in the shooting houses. Shooter X can slowly place a full 30-round M4 or AK-47 magazine into a target with a group less than 2 inches in diameter from 25 meters away. He is well trained in the basic steps of marksmanship; stance, grip, trigger control, sight alignment, and follow-through. But going into a shooting house and distinguishing between non-threats and threats, shooting while moving, and shouting commands to the non-threats is a completely different story.

As Bruce Siddle explains in *Sharpening the Warrior's Edge,* a person fighting to stay alive must be competent to perform under high levels of stress and arousal. The unconsciously competent individual begins responding appropriately as he first becomes aware of the threat. For this reason, people who have experienced a deadly encounter are sometimes unable to describe the exact, step-by-step process by which they defended themselves. Many times people will simply say something to the effect of, "I recognized the person to be a threat, I aimed at center mass and I continued to squeeze off rounds until the threat was neutralized." For the modern day gunslinger, that is considered a successful outcome.

HANDGUNS

"I know not with what weapons World War III will be fought, but World War IV will be fought with sticks and stones."
—Albert Einstein

The art and science of self-defense handgunning has been continuously evolving and improving for over two hundred years. And for the last fifty years or so, its developmental pace has increased dramatically. Citizens' awareness of the need for effective self-defense has burgeoned, possibly due to the rapid decay of our cities, an increase in crime, the global spread of terrorism, deteriorating social conditions, and economic concerns. It isn't surprising at all that so many people are concerned with home and personal defense. It is actually somewhat rare to hear of anyone *not* concerned with personal and home defense.

Home defense can take many forms—electronic security systems, video surveillance, infrared, seismic detectors, dogs, etc. Yet, even these defenses are often circumvented. Regardless of what other measures you take, in order to be safe, time and energy should also be invested in the more personal aspects of the defense issue—the use of "deadly force."

Though many people believe that the shotgun/long gun may be the home defense weapon of choice, the small size, ease of storage, and relatively simple operational characteristics of the handgun make it the most practical and popular alternative for most people.

Firearms provide capabilities unique among other common types of weapons. The most obvious of these is range. With empty hands, or with a contact weapon such as a club or a knife, you have to be essentially within arm's reach to strike the threat without moving your feet.

As mentioned earlier in the text, most situations requiring the use of deadly force in self-defense occur at close ranges. A handgun will allow you to strike effectively from an almost unlimited variety of angles and body positions, even if you are injured, sick, or tired. A handgun is also a good weapon to use when there is something such as a piece of furniture between you and your target, since there is no need to close the gap. Provided that a vital area is hit, the striking power of a firearm is the same for every user. If you can see your threat, you can do serious harm to him, and he knows it.

Even though our intended shot placement areas include center mass, the pelvis, and the head, a handgun allows you to damage a wide range of body targets. This is also possible if the threat is hidden behind something. Physically, it takes little effort to use a gun. Knives demand more effort to use than guns. Psychologically guns are harder to use than clubs but easier than knives. The use of knives require a good deal of attention and conditioning to overcome natural aversions (which is one of the reasons why firearms were developed). Empty-hand techniques typically are also physically and psychologically demanding.

Firearms do have several limitations. First, the legalities of owning and carrying a gun for self-defense can vary greatly, depending on where you live. For example, in New York and Washington, D.C., handgun ownership is greatly restricted or even prohibited; in New Hampshire, Florida, and Washington State, any law-abiding citizen without a criminal record or history of mental instability can easily obtain a permit for a concealed weapon. In Arizona and New Mexico, handguns may be carried openly in a holster without any license at all. However, in many jurisdictions, legal possession of a loaded firearm is often limited to one's home, business, or private property.

In contrast to many other weapons, firearms always constitute the use of deadly force. "Shooting to wound" only happens in the movies. If you weren't in danger for your life how would you justify using a gun in the first place?

The handgun was designed to be used at close range or what we call "conversational distance." And it has been used with great success in close range battle since its inception.

When choosing a handgun you have a wide variety to choose from—everything from the famed six-shooter revolvers of the Wild West, to state-of-the-art hand-crafted race guns used in IPSC matches, to the reliable Glock you'll find in many law enforcement, military, or government holsters throughout the world.

Factors to Consider When Choosing a Handgun:

- Compromise between the power of a weapon's round and the size of the weapon
- Ease with which you can control that power
- Size for concealment
- Ease with which you can operate, load, reload, and unload the weapon.
- Feel of weapon, which you want to be comfortable thus enhancing performance and reducing errors.
- Can you work the trigger without seriously disturbing sight alignment?
- Can you can readily get the muzzle realigned with your intended target for follow-up shots?

Handguns offer plenty of advantages due to their concealability, portability, and maneuverability. But they only fire relatively small rounds. If you work or live in an area where you more or less can expect trouble, you may want to consider a weapon that doesn't sacrifice too much firepower, e.g., a shotgun.

Many newer shooters allow others to make their decision on what gun to buy, via articles, classes, or discussions. The fact is that gun owners' lifestyles and needs are different. What works for one person may not work for another, so consider your needs carefully before purchasing a weapon.

Revolvers vs. Semiautomatics

Your handgun choices basically boil down to two primary options: the revolver or the semiautomatic pistol. They both have their advantages and disadvantages. The revolver tends to be slower to operate for all but the very fastest revolver shooters, but is very accurate and can still be perfectly adequate depending on your needs. The semiautomatic, for most shooters, is much quicker for most but not necessarily as reliable.

A single- or double-action semiautomatic pistol will fit the needs of most shooters. In a single-action weapon, a light, short movement of the trigger fires the weapon that is already cocked; in a double-action gun, a heavier, longer trigger movement first cocks the hammer or striker and then releases it, firing the weapon. The light trigger press of a single-action weapon is obviously easier than the heavier roll of a double-action trigger, although it is easier to discharge a single-action weapon unintentionally. However, the "startle reaction" can be more than enough to fire a double-action weapon as well.

The single-action semi is the easiest to shoot as the long, heavy double-action semi trigger pull required to fire the first shot takes a lot more time with the trigger pull. This is perhaps the double-action semi's biggest weakness.

Two-handed revolver grip

The double-action revolver is another viable option. In concept, it's by far the simplest and thus carries much merit, especially for the novice shooter.

The problem is that the double-action revolver can only be used quickly when in the double-action trigger-cocked mode since trigger control is everything! Although it's a simple weapon to understand, the double-action revolver and semi are tougher to shoot than a single-action semi.

Pistols with a shorter-barreled sight radius are more difficult to use effectively (except for point-shooting). The closer the front and rear sites are to one another, the more alignment errors you'll have.

The shorter barrel also limits bullet velocities, which reduces the weapon's efficiency.

You should not simply select a handgun simply because it has a large-capacity magazine. The dynamics of defensive handgun confrontations follow a trend—they're close (usually less than three meters) and they're fast (usually in less than three seconds), so you will not usually have time to shoot much anyway unless you sacrifice accuracy.

Do not discount the revolver just because it only holds five to seven rounds. It is the weapon I chose for my wife since she does not shoot often and there is very little you need to know about a revolver in order to shoot it. They have been around in more or less their current form for over a hundred years and have a good efficiency record.

Likewise, don't pick a handgun that's too powerful for you to handle under stress. Combat shooting involves both speed and combat accuracy—so weapon control is crucial.

Ensure your weapon has sights you can see quickly at high speed, but are low profile to prevent snagging in clothing.

You want to have a clean, crisp trigger; a 3 ½–6 lbs. trigger pull is about right.

A good two-handed grip. Time for a speed re-load.

> **Note:** Approximately 30 percent of people shot with a handgun die, while 70 percent of those shot with a shotgun or a center-fire rifle die.

If a person is not going to shoot more than a few times a year, a revolver might actually be the weapon of choice. A semi may offer certain advantages, such as greater ammunition capacity and a lighter trigger pull, but again, it's more complicated to operate.

If you require more than 5–7 rounds, generally it can be said that you've got a shooting problem, not a capacity problem. A revolver should provide plenty of ammunition considering that the average defender in a gunfight fires approximately three rounds. Of course you should always have a speed re-loader or at least additional ammunition ready to load, if needed.

You'll be glad you had spare ammo or maybe a couple of speed re-loaders if there are multiple assailants; if any of them are moving or partially behind cover; if there is diminshed light; or if you have to lay down cover fire to enable a retreat.

Many folks question why revolvers still remain in existence. If you can carry a semi, why carry a revolver?

Chuck Taylor, the first four-weapon combat master and former world class IPSC competitor, points out that an interesting trend began in the early 1980s. Around this time confrontations by law enforcement officers with armed felons took a serious turn—officers who had always felt sufficiently armed suddenly felt outgunned.

There was no question something had changed. In comparison with long-established norms, law enforcement shootings began to skyrocket. Police officers began to encounter more sophisticated weapons like those carried by military personnel.

As a result, the law-enforcement community decided they lacked "firepower" and that the weapons of the criminals in the street were superior to theirs. And before long, the revolver used by most law enforcement officers was becoming obsolete.

In its place the Beretta M92 began to appear in the holsters of police officers and military personnel as well. A wide variety of semis immediately followed the already well-known .45 M1911, Browning Hi-Power, and Beretta into the marketplace.

Pistols with large magazine capacity were especially favored, since they allowed shooters to carry as many as 20 rounds in their weapons, which did much to level the "firepower" playing field.

The civilian shooting community, which had always followed trends set by law enforcement and the military, became vastly aware that the day of the revolver was past. After all, law enforcement and the military always used the state-of-the-art weapons. Revolver sales dropped drastically, while semi sales soared.

It looked like the day of the revolver had passed. But over the years revolvers began to reappear in gun shops and trade shows. By the end of 1999, they'd risen back to levels deemed to be at least adequate to continue production.

A collection of semiautomatics

For most shooters the revolver is a fully capable weapon and since its inception in 1831 it has done quite well as a defensive weapon.

In comparison with the semi, the revolver does theoretically lack "firepower." But it's a proven fact that large magazines often cause people to shoot faster than they can hit. And "firepowering" a threat into submission isn't faster than two or three quick, effective shots.

If you hit what you shoot at, the revolver's five or seven rounds is plenty. As an old-time western marshal once said, "After I've fired five rounds from my single-action Colt .45, I have all the time in the world to reload!"

There are many shooters who feel more comfortable with a revolver because they like its inherent simplicity. The concept of the semi intimidates some novice shooters who don't want to bother with sophisticated loading, unloading, press-checks, or malfunctions.

Note the muzzle flip and the spent brass in the air.

Police conducting handgun training in full combat gear.

Compacts and Subcompacts

Compact and subcompact handguns have become very popular in the last two-plus decades. Nearly every kind of standard-sized pistol now has at least a smaller counterpart.

If you want a pistol capable of high performance in all kinds of tactical situations, then you want a general purpose full-sized handgun. But if your needs are more specialized, such as having a concealed, reasonably effective handgun for specific types of defensive scenarios, the compact and sub-compact may be more appropriate options.

Law enforcement and military personnel need a pistol capable of handling a wide range of tactical scenarios. A civilian does not. Compacts and sub-compacts are perfectly good weapons when they're used within their limitations, just like any other tool.

Compact and subcompacts have a significantly shorter sight radius, which makes fast sight acquisition and alignment more difficult. Also, their shorter barrels produce lower bullet velocities, which means bullet expansion is less likely. Their lighter weight means more recoil and muzzle flip and, in many cases (depending upon the cartridge involved) a sharper recoil impulse. However, their smaller size and lighter weight make them much easier to carry and conceal and they generally perform well as defensive weapons.

The shorter sight radius of the compact/subcompact isn't such a disadvantage in situations where the threat will be engaged at less than approximately 20 feet. Compacts and subcompacts can produce the accuracy needed for self-defense. In fact, nearly all models shoot far more accurately than anyone can operate them.

There is a misconceptions that compacts/subcompacts are intrinsically inaccurate. This stems from the fact that the older versions, like the old Colt Pocket Model, tend to be so small that they're nearly impossible to hold properly, making consistent weapon control a problem. They either have sights so small that they're virtually useless or no sights at all.

Modern compact/subcompacts are sufficiently large to allow for decent hand placement and usually have the same high-visibility fixed sights as full-size pistols, making them much easier to shoot well.

DEFENSIVE HANDGUN AMMUNITION

It almost goes without saying that when you are choosing handgun ammunition, you should select only the recommended ammunition for that weapon. Some ammunition is better used for training and some is better suited for defensive purposes. This chapter discusses some of the criteria to consider when choosing your ammunition.

The most significant issue with the selection of a handgun is the caliber and the wounding effectiveness of ammunition. Research has proven that people receiving even fatal injuries have been able to "stay in the fight" and return fire. As a defensive shooter, your objective is to remove the threat's ability to "stay in the fight."

Incapacitation results from psychological and/or physiological factors. It is rare but due to psychological responses some people simply go right into condition black and become incapacitated when shot regardless of the severity of the wound(s). Others continue to fight even though they are seriously or even fatally wounded. Much of this has to do with the combat mind-set of the individual. Because a person's psychological response to a gunshot wound cannot be predicted, ammunition performance must be viewed from the perspective of physiological incapacitation.

Because the placement of a shot in the head can be somewhat difficult and cannot be counted upon, a round must penetrate the body sufficiently to rupture major arteries and/or blood-filled organs to ensure a timely physiological incapacitation.

Given adequate penetration, the only reliable way to increase the effectiveness of the wound is to increase its size, which increases the amount of tissue damage and the rate of hemorrhage. But keep in mind—larger rounds are heavier to carry and add to the recoil effect of the weapon.

Terminal Performance

Terminal performance refers to a type of ammunition's ability to stop a threat by penetrating the threat's body deep enough while also protecting innocent parties by not exiting the threat. Most shooters rely on hollow points to maximize terminal performance from handguns. The opening in a hollow point round typically fills with blood, fluid, tissue, and clothing, which aid in the round's expansion. Hollow points are generally the best choice for all-around handgun self-defense.

Most handgun rounds will go through most urban structures, e.g., sheet-rock walls, hollow-core doors, wooden door frames, etc., which is a problem if there are other individuals in the house or building. The list is long of those who have been killed by a round going through a wall and into an unintended person. As a matter of fact, I have two friends to whom this occurred. One of them fell to the floor when the round went through the wall. He immediately did not understand why he fell, but he has been in a wheel chair ever since. The round perforated his spinal cord. Another friend of mine was not so lucky. He took two unintended rounds, which came through a wall, accidentally. He was struck between the gap in his body armor, and the rounds damaged both kidneys, both lungs, and his heart. He died a slow and painful death.

There are pre-fragmented or partially pre-fragmented rounds available. They may be the round of choice in environments where there is an abnormally high risk of over-penetration, such as a home, however they may not always provide enough penetration to be effective.

Handgun rounds typically do not generate the high velocities required to yield true hydrostatic shock. The larger diameter the round, the better the chance of it hitting major blood vessels and/or organs. The small, temporary stretch channel in the soft tissue created by these relatively low-velocity rounds does not contribute much to incapacitation. A person struck by a handgun round is not likely to be stunned by neural shock, which is the temporary disruption of the central nervous system resulting from trauma. It typically causes the person to collapse and pass out.

Handgun rounds typically incapacitate people either by striking the central nervous system (the "fatal T") or by perforating the heart, blood-filled organs, or any other major blood vessels, causing significant blood loss.

The "one-shot" stop should never be counted on, regardless of the weapon or ammunition used. Multiple shots fired into a person, as quickly as possible, will create more "leak points" and thus increase the chance of hitting vital areas in the body.

Most law enforcement and military throughout the world carry 9mm pistols, although the U.S. forces fighting in Iraq and Afghanistan are very dissatisfied with them and have welcomed the return of the larger .45 round. Although smaller, the 9x19mm round still has the capacity to penetrate the skull and damage the pelvic bone. In 9mm the best results have been with hollow points in the 115–127 +P grain loads.

A .40 cal is a bigger and higher powered round than a 9mm, making it harder to shoot accurately because of its increased recoil forces.

The .38 Specials have shown the best results with the 125–158 +P grain. The gold standard for handgun ammunition has been the 125 grain, .357 Magnum semi-jacketed hollow point. The lighter and slower 110-grain loads are a good alternative to the 125-grain.

You can fire a .357-caliber handgun most economically by training with the .38 Specials. The weapon actually operates with either .357 Magnum or .38 Specials, but the .357 ammunition is more costly than the .38. In combat, on the street or in home defense, I would highly recommend carrying the .357 Magnum rounds, despite the cost.

In .45 caliber, the Federal's .45 ACP Hydra-Shok, 230-grain weight perform as well as the high-velocity 125-grain.

The wad cutter is an inexpensive, flat-based lead round that is an excellent choice for target practice. The semi-wad cutter is a tapered lead bullet. These bullets come in different grain weights. The higher the grain weight, the more recoil you'll feel since the higher the grain, the heavier the bullet.

A full-metal-jacket round is another relatively inexpensive round for handgun target shooting since it does not expand. This round is popular in 9 mm, .40-caliber, and .45-caliber automatic pistols.

The jacketed soft-point ammunition performs well on the range and also works well for defensive purposes. One of the most expensive rounds would be a jacketed hollow-point round. This is an expanding bullet, normally used for self-defense.

Double-Stack vs. Single-Stack Magazines

For those with smaller hands the bulkiness of most semi grips, like the Glock, due to their double stack configuration, makes for a poor grip. On some weapons the grips can be customized and made slimmer.

There has been very little data indicating the need for high capacity or bulky magazines. In very few cases have more than five shots been fired in a handgun shootout. And with few exceptions,

Glock offers an extended magazine, which works very well as a backup mag.

there has not been the need for a reload to continue a fight. The exceptions include the infamous Miami and North Hollywood shootouts, in which a multitude of rounds were fired.

The FBI Miami shootout was a 1986 gun battle between eight FBI agents and two heavily armed and well-trained gunmen. Two special agents were killed, as well as the two robbery suspects. Despite outnumbering the suspects 4 to 1, the FBI agents found themselves pinned down by rifle fire and unable to respond effectively. Although both were hit several times in the battle, one fought on and continued to injure and kill the officers.

The 1997 North Hollywood shootout was an another armed confrontation between two heavily armed and armored bank robbers and L.A. patrol and SWAT officers. It happened when responding officers engaged the suspects after they robbed a bank. Ten officers and seven civilians sustained injuries before both robbers were killed.

Shooting Maxims

"The three most important components of stopping power are: bullet placement, bullet placement, and bullet placement."

—Evan Marshall

"One hundred rounds do not constitute firepower. One hit constitutes firepower."

—General Merritt Edson, U.S.MC

MARKSMANSHIP

The Complete Shooter

Although marksmanship is a critical component, it is only one-third of the complete shooter's triangle. Tactics and combat mindset must also be emphasized unless all you want to do is bull's-eye shooting. A great deal of professional basic weapons training focuses solely on marksmanship, ignoring the fact that shooters must go well beyond shooting at stationary targets from stationary positions.

There is a distinct difference between the target shooter and the combat shooter. The target shooter is concerned with a tight group. The combat shooter is concerned with achieving "combat accuracy" and neutralizing threats.

Training Tip: Statistics show that 95 percent of law enforcement officers that hit their target with the first shot will go home. If the first shot misses, the number drops to 48 percent Most law enforcement miss 75–80 percent of shots fired in lethal force encounters. Fortunately, law enforcement studies show that the "bad guys" hit their intended target only 14 percent of the time.

Shooter's Triangle

Training Tip: Loss of mental concentration degrades marksmanship. Avoid "brain fade." Once you begin to lose concentration while training on the range, take a break.

Although impressive in its own way, I am usually only somewhat interested when I see a shooter training on the range, standing at the 7-yard line and firing round after round from the ready position into the same silver dollar-size hole. This is notable because this shooter has obviously mastered some of the basics of marksmanship, e.g., trigger control and sight alignment. He apparently understands how his weapon functions and is obviously very accurate. But as striking as this may be to a casual observer, or even to the shooter himself, if this is all he trains to do, then at the very best he can be considered only one-third of the "complete shooter."

*Richard Belmore, South Carolina Law Enforcement
Division, concealed weapons instructor, training with "funny face" targets.*

The complete shooter has trained and spent considerable time doing more than just mastering the basic shooting fundamentals. He has practiced tactics and developed a combat mind-set. He utilizes a holistic approach toward training, one that merges the physical and mental elements together.

For a shooter to become and stay proficient a great deal of ongoing training must take place on and off the range. Shooting, like most disciplines, is a perishable skill. Although time, space, and financial constraints can prevent many of us from training as we wish, it is up to each of us to stay proficient with our shooting. If getting out to the range is not always an option, practice dry fire,

Kelly Armenta, weapons instructor, at the range. Photos courtesy of Richard Belmore.

utilize visualization techniques, read all that you can find on the subject, watch shooting training videos, etc.

> **Training Tip:** Learn your natural point of aim (NPOA).

Combat Accuracy

Being able to quickly hit an eight-inch circle from wherever you are is considered *combat accuracy*. Being able to shoot a tight group into a target using well-aimed, slow fire is target shooting. There is a big difference between the two. Target shooting is a necessary part of training but as defensive shooters, we are mostly concerned with being able to deliver quick shots with combat accuracy.

Many fights have been won because the winner's first shots put the loser behind the power curve. Hits anywhere—center mass, head, or pelvis—delivered as fast as possible, win gunfights.

Combat accuracy does not require tight groups. All that is required to stop a threat with handgun rounds are hits to the central nervous system and/or hits that drop the blood pressure with large and/or numerous cardiovascular system injuries.

The Fundamentals of Marksmanship

To better your chances of achieving combat accuracy, your goal should be to try to master the fundamentals of marksmanship. By definition, marksmanship consists of a critically important set of skills that need to be developed and fine-tuned in order for a shooter to become competent. There are five basic fundamentals to marksmanship: stance, grip, sight alignment, trigger control, and

> **Training Tip:** The complete shooter is well rounded in marksmanship, tactics, and combat mind-set. There may not be much in common between range training and a gunfight, but a substantial foundation in marksmanship and a bit on tactics can be acquired on a range.

Photos courtesy of Officer Chris Geary, York County Police Dept.

follow-through. Whether you're a college student, housewife, SWAT member, Navy SEAL, or a competitive shooter vying for an Olympic medal, these basic shooting fundamentals remain the same.

Marksmanship skills should be practiced as close to "perfect" as possible—I can't stress that enough. Practice only creates habits, but perfect practice makes perfect. The conscious mind does not work well at times of stress. The subconscious, the nonanalytical portion of the mind, which is influenced with repetitive training,

works much better under stress. It is the subconscious that is capable of performing a "hard-wired" technique that you have ingrained with countless (at least 1,500–3,000) perfect repetitions. You will fight like you have trained, so how you train is critical.

Training Tip: The insatiable human desire for instant gratification—not focusing on the front sight but looking for the bullet's impact before the firing cycle is complete—will cause you to watch your misses.

Note: Reports have indicated that U.S. law enforcement officers average only about 20 percent hits during gunfights, which means they miss about 80 percent of the time. There are many factors that can explain this but on

Range training. Photos courtesy of Government Training Institute Inc.

top of that list is the fact that they frequently do not receive the amount of marksmanship training they require—in particular, training that simulates life-or-death scenarios.

Basic marksmanship fundamentals will be described in detail in the chapters that follow.

Shooting Maxims

"We continue to be amused by people who feel that shot group diameter on paper is an end in itself. I can always get a perfect shot group. All I have to do is fire just one shot."—Louis Awerbuck

"Speed's fine but accuracy is final."

—Bill Jordan

"Speed is five-sixths smoothness."

—Ray Chapman

"Take the time you need to make the shot but don't waste any time."

—Peter Samish

"The most important lesson I learned . . . was that the winner of a gunfight usually was the one who took his time."

—Wyatt Earp

"The secret in winning a gunfight is taking your time in a hurry."

—Wyatt Earp

STANCE

The Shooter's Stance

Being a complete shooter requires much more than being able to shoot at a target from the standing position. Being able to effectively use a variety of positions greatly expands your ability to deliver effective, well-aimed fire while minimizing your exposure by using available cover.

There are literally dozens of stances and variations for each of the common shooting stances. This is because everybody is built differently. What works well for you may not work quite as well for another shooter. If a particular stance works well for someone whose basic body shape and proportions are similar to yours, it's possible that the same basic stance will work well for you. But because your body is not identical to his, you will probably still have to tweak the stance a little to make it *your* stance.

Any stance will work when discharging a firearm. You can literally stand on your head and shoot or you can bend over and shoot between your legs—they all work. But some work better than others and if you are diligent enough you will experiment and find the stance that works best for you.

Every time you fire your weapon your body is in *some* kind of stance (hopefully the one you have practiced most often). One of the many benefits of practicing perfect practice is that when you have perfected the stance that works for you and you utilize this

> **Training Tip:** Develop a natural and instinctive point of aim (NPOA). In combat or defensive shooting, a tight group is not important.

stance in your training, then when it comes time to shift into condition red in a life-threatening situation, you will unconsciously go to the stance you have practiced so often—the one that has proven to work best for you.

A good shooting stance, be it for pistol, rifle, or shotgun fire, requires *stability, mobility,* and *balance.* Ideally, a stance also includes the natural point of aim (NPOA).

- Stability: Stability is gained by using a forward center of gravity and balance, often referred to as an aggressive fighting stance or a forward aggressive lean. If the shooter is inadvertently bumped by another person, the shooter should be stable enough not to fall out of position. Recoil from the shooting is also absorbed passively with a good stable stance. This is more critical when it comes to rapid fire and automatic fire.
- Mobility: Mobility is something you really do not want to give up if you can avoid it. You want to be able to quickly move into and out of positions, to be ready to quickly fire or to shoot on the move while obtaining combat accuracy. Granted, you may have to give up some mobility based on your available cover, but if you do not have to give it up—don't. One exception: snipers do a great deal of their shooting from a prone position, but they are the masters when it comes to the use of cover and concealment.
- Balance: Your balance will determine how soon you will be ready to shoot when moving or getting into or out of positions. An

awkward shooting position can adversely affect your balance. Many novice shooters often lose their balance when standing or kneeling behind cover. When standing, keep your weight forward of your center of gravity by standing on the balls of your feet. This will allow for better absorption of energy from the recoil and multiple shots. Lean slightly forward from the hips in an aggressive posture. Your rear foot will help to maintain your fore and aft balance and will provide a great base in order to quickly mobilize from. You stance has to allow you to shoot and move rapidly.

NPOA (Natural Point of Aim): Whenever possible maintain your "natural point of aim" while shooting. The NPOA is something you will learn to incorporate with experience. It is the way in which you orient your body, arm, and wrist so they remain in an aiming position without any muscular effort or correction. Your NPOA should be maintained using only skeletal support. Once you establish your NPOA, you can glance away without losing your aim. As much as

possible, incorporate NPOA into your stances until it feels natural. Eliminate, or at least minimize, muscle tension in your body. This will result in better performance and is much less fatiguing. A good stance does not require any muscular tension. The push-pull methods (e.g., the Weaver Stance) require muscular support which is another drawback for this stance.

The most common shooting positions include lying prone (on your chest), lying on your back or either side, kneeling, sitting, squatting, and standing. All of these positions have their advantages and all have their disadvantages.

The more stability you have the less mobility you will have and vice versa. A standing shooter basically has a platform consisting of only his own two feet. He has an excellent opportunity for quick movement (mobility) but is not very stable or balanced compared to a kneeling or prone position. A person in the prone position has great balance and stability but very little mobility.

Shooting Positions

It was once stated that any shooter who concentrates on getting into a good stance in a firefight has taken too much time doing so.

Author utilizing available cover

Shooter using a van as cover.
Right: Jon F., range instructor, shooting behind the engine block.

The key is not to have to think about it. Through perfect practice—repetition, repetition, repetition—your body will go to this perfect stance when the time comes.

The situations in which a weapon is used vary widely and can greatly influence the particular stance adopted by the shooter. Maintaining a variety of stances will make you a more effective shooter.

Over the years I have seen shooting stances and techniques demonstrated in countless different ways. The ideal shooting stance is one in which you can effectively fire your weapon and hopefully remain behind some cover or concealment. If all you have for cover is a roadside curb or fire hydrant, you may be forced to fire from the prone position. You may be behind a wheel and engine block (safest cover if around a vehicle) and then you would have an option to change your shooting profile and vary from one shooting position and/or location to another.

If the threat sees you shooting from the same position for too long, it will not be long before he can gain a tactical advantage over you. So, when possible, change positions, move from cover to cover and do not remain a static target. If you are behind a wheel and engine block, your options would include shooting from the prone (under the vehicle), kneeling (in front of the vehicle) or squatting (over the hood) positions and looking for your next cover, perhaps another vehicle or behind a building.

> **Note:** Before leaving cover and going to another position, reload (tactical reload if possible). You do not want to be caught without ammunition while running from cover to cover.

Evolution of Pistol Stances

During the early 1960s Jeff Cooper, the father of modern pistolcraft, along with Bill Jordan, Chic Gaylord, Jack Weaver, Elden Carl, Thell Reed, John Plahn, and Ray Chapman, founded the Southwest Combat Pistol League (SWCPL) in Big Bear, California. Jack Weaver's technique, the Weaver Stance, became the predominant technique used by these and other top shooters. Those using this technique were winning most of the early pistol shooting competitions. Weaver's new stance simply proved to be superior to the traditional one-handed techniques.

The SWCPL soon change its name to the Southwest Pistol League (SWPL). The name change was forced because the word "combat" was politically incorrect, even back then.

The founding members of the SWCPL, and subsequent SWPL, were at that time considered to be the best shooters in the country. The SWPL became very important in the shooting world, and shaped the entire shooting community in the ensuing years.

In the mid-1970s, Jeff Cooper and others from the SWPL founded the International Practical Shooting Confederation. When it was first formed, IPSC was designed to be a test bed for combat shooting techniques, equipment, and mind-set. All the equipment used in these competitions was defensive-type gear. The matches themselves were designed with defensive tactics in mind. This would later change, and IPSC would become a pure shooting competition where high-tech, competition-style gear, including compensators and optical sights, would come to rule.

Years later, Rob Leatham and Brian Enos arrived on the IPSC shooting scene. They blew away the rest of the competition by using the new Modern Isosceles stance and forever changed the IPSC and the shooting world.

Today, all of the top IPSC shooters, most law enforcement departments, and most military units use the Modern Isosceles stance. Many in the martial arts community still use the Weaver technique or a modified version of it so that it works with their hybrid teaching of martial arts and weapons.

Author giving a shooting demonstration

Weaver Stance

Tradition held for many years that shooters would fire from their hip or shoulder, but rarely would they use both hands to shoot a pistol. In the 1950s, L.A. County deputy sheriff Jack Weaver made popular a two-handed shooting stance that still bears his name today—the Weaver Stance. The stance was named after Jack Weaver although he did not create it; the shooting technique had actually been around for quite some time before he started using it.

As revolutionary as it was at the time, it's actually pretty basic: simply use both hands to hold and support the weapon, with your elbows bent, and the dominant arm pushing while the support hand pulls. The excitement and challenge of wide-open pistol competition led Deputy Weaver to develop the stance, with the sole purpose of winning Jeff Cooper's "Leatherslap" competition in Big Bear, California. Over time, almost everyone in the shooting community began using the Weaver Stance.

Chapman Stance (Modified Weaver)

The Chapman Stance, named for renowned shooter Ray Chapman, used the same push-pull tension as the Weaver, but instead of both elbows being bent, the gunside elbow is held straight and locked in place. Assuming a right-handed shooter, the right arm is punched straight out, while the left elbow is bent and the left hand pulls back to provide tension. As a result of this change, the Chapman gets its stability from both muscle and skeletal support.

This technique has advantages and disadvantage. The body is bladed somewhat, making for a potentially smaller target when facing a threat; however, when wearing body armor, blading your body toward a threat exposes your center mass—which is not covered by armor. Many law enforcement departments and the military trained this way for years. Jeff Cooper taught SEAL teams this method in the early 1980s.

A young Brion Enos, one of the greatest shooters of our time

This shooter is not practicing a good forward aggressive stance.

The problem that many experienced with this technique was that many shooters did not automatically respond to a threat by going into this stance, regardless of the number of repetitions they practiced. It was unnatural. The push-pull method requires an awkward sequence of steps, and does not work well when covering a room or open space. A right-handed shooter can easily cover to his right but it is difficult to cover a full 180 degrees to his left side. It is also awkward to go from a Weaver or Chapman stance directly to a kneeling or prone position.

Shooters, more times than not, reverted to a natural action stance when confronted by a threat, heard a loud noise, an explosion, or a gunshot. The body did not naturally go to a Weaver or

Chapman stance. It was a losing battle trying to teach shooters to switch the hardwire of the brain and not to go into a natural action stance instinctively.

When teaching shooting courses I would often ask a shooter to come up to the front of class and would, without warning, throw something at him. More often than not he would go into the natural action stance to catch it. When up close to a threat, people reverted to this stance. The natural action stance seemed to be the best base to work from in creating the optimum shooting stance. The Modified Isosceles stance closely resembles the natural action stance, which is already hardwired into the subconscious.

Modified Isosceles Stance

Like most instructors, this is the only stance I now teach to shooters as the primary defensive handgun shooting stance. Depending on the experience level of the class or student, I introduce the other stances as well. It is important to have a variety of tools in your tactical toolbox, but if you have too many choices, it will slow down your reaction time.

Most of the shooters trained in the Weaver or Chapman stance revert to the Modified (or Modern) Isosceles stance when faced with unexpected life-threatening situations. This is to be expected since instinct takes over during the fight or flight mode.

In defensive shooting, we face our threat relatively "squarely," meaning that both shoulders will be similarly distant from the perceived threat. This also places our poorly defensible backs away from the threat.

Bring the weapon to your midline because in this position it tends to be placed under the nose, in line with the eyes. Your arms will approximate the legs of an isosceles triangle, with your chest forming its base. Your line of sight will closely parallel the altitude of the triangle, but keep in mind that if the barrel of the weapon is aligned with the bones of your forearm, it will extend the leg of the triangle past its apex, pointing off to your non-dominant side.

In the Modified Isosceles, both arms are close to full extension. This puts the axis of recoil more or less along the centerline of the body. Train with the non-gun-side foot slightly forward. The dominant-side foot is approximately half a foot length behind the non-dominant foot and the body leans slightly forward from the hip ready to mobilize if situation dictates. The back of the foot helps with fore and aft stability and balance.

Defensive shooting positions should not require any major head movement to acquire the sights. The head should not have to move to the sights—the sights are brought up to eye level.

The best way to manage recoil is to make sure that your shoulders are forward of your hips when you fire. This position is easily accomplished by relaxing the ankles, knees, and hips with a slight forward lean, but not enough to put you off balance.

While Weaver, Chapman, and the Modified Isosceles are the most popular defensive handgun stances, they are not the only ones. The handgun stances listed below also work and sometimes work better than the Modified Isosceles, given the circumstances.

Off-Handed Shooting Stance

One- and two-handed shooting techniques must be incorporated into your training. A two-handed stance is certainly optimal from the standpoint of weapon stability, trigger control, and recoil management. However, in the real world, situations often arise in which it is necessary or desirable to shoot with just one hand. For instance, your support hand may be injured, occupied, opening a door, or pushing a non-threat out of the way.

There is significant evidence from real world shooting cases that many people shoot one-handed under stress, even if they have been taught to shoot with both hands. In particular, reacting to a close-range threat seems to elicit this response, especially if the shooter is moving or surprised.

Officer Jan W. practicing off-handed shooting.

U.S. law enforcement reports indicate at least half of quick-reaction shootings occur one-handed, particularly at ranges less than 7 yards.

One-handed shooting takes two primary forms: visually verified fire from eye level, and unsighted shooting at contact distance from a weapon retention position. These variations address different tactical situations and require completely different techniques.

Eye-level shooting is for situations not within arm's reach. Naturally, the following discussion on grip, sight alignment, trigger control, and follow-through still applies. Grip is also the same since it's impractical to have one grip for two-handed shooting and another when firing with one hand unsupported.

Another technique is to reach behind your back, grip the weapon, and withdraw it from the holster. Some may not be able to make this reach. Make sure when you do this that you keep the muzzle pointing away from the body or at least in a safe direction (pointed down or to the rear). Bring the weapon around to the support side of the body.

Author in the "fallen officer" position

Author giving a shooting demonstration of a wounded hand simulation.

Lean forward to create an over-balance in the direction you are firing in order to counter the recoil. You may wish to rotate your torso to put your weapon side forward. Ideal foot placement will therefore be gun-side foot to the front.

To further minimize shot-to-shot recovery time, bring the weapon to the position where muscle tension is your NPOA. The weapon will then come back to the NPOA without additional effort on your part. You can find this point in practice by observing the path the front sight travels as the weapon discharges, then rotating your hand after every few shots until you locate the place where the weapon returns on target after recoil.

Shooting from the Modified Isosceles stance actually enhances the ability to shoot with the dominant or the non-dominant hand unsupported, since both arms extend in a mirror image in the two-handed stance.

A contact-distance, weapon-retention position is the other one-handed technique that belongs in every gunslinger's tactical toolbox. Even the earliest of the combat gunslingers recognized the necessity of keeping the weapon close to the body when in close proximity to a threat.

Unfortunately, most "hip-shooting" techniques do not take into account the physically violent nature of a close quarters fight.

Place your non-shooting hand on the center of your chest when training in one-handed shooting techniques. This keeps it in position to strike or block an incoming attack in a close-quarters confrontation.

Support-Hand Presentation

Oftentimes you may hear the support hand referred to as the weak hand. I prefer "support" or "non-dominant" rather than weak. Most of us do not or should not have weak hands. Our support hand or non-dominant hand supports our shooting hand. However, our support hand may end up being our shooting hand in case of injury; when you find yourself in an awkward shooting position; or when the shooting arm is occupied or holding on to something to prevent a fall.

Research has shown that many people have been shot in the hand while holding their weapon. People generally shoot what they look at—the weapon. On the range, most of the "funny face" targets are holding weapons, and it is the weapons that are shot, rather than center mass. Once a person sees a weapon, they often just shoot at that weapon and skip the critical step of bringing their weapon up to the threat's center mass.

Remember you're empowered to protect yourself at all times, not just when the situation is the one you're

most comfortable with. A competent shooter can shoot, reload, and correct malfunctions with either hand acting alone.

Unless these skills are regularly practiced, they will not feel comfortable nor will they be as effective.

One of the problems in executing a support-hand presentation is the initial establishment of a good grip. Below are some methods that are commonly used by some of the top pistol shooters.

Reach with the support hand across the front of the torso and grip the weapon in a sort of reverse cross-draw, then withdraw it in

a rolling motion across the torso while simultaneously attempting to obtain an adequate grip.

This is often a difficult procedure unless practiced regularly. As you may imagine, there is chance that the weapon will be dropped as it rolls across the torso.

Procedures for conducting a one-handed reload or malfunction clearing:

One-handed reload

One of the many reasons I like the Glock is because it does not have external safeties. If your pistol has an external safety you will have to manipulate the safety selector with your support hand and this will most likely be difficult since it would require the use of a fine motor skill.

With weapons training we try to stay with techniques that require only gross motor skill involvement. Fine motor skills often disappear when under stress, and the likelihood is that with most shooters, having to defend themselves with a pistol with their support hand will create some level of stress.

Slidelock

Weapon at the ready position

Slide lock

Remove the magazine

Magazine clear

Holster weapon

Reach for new magazine

Insert magazine into magazine well

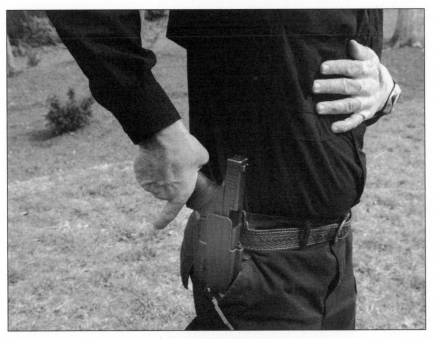

Ensure magazine is seated

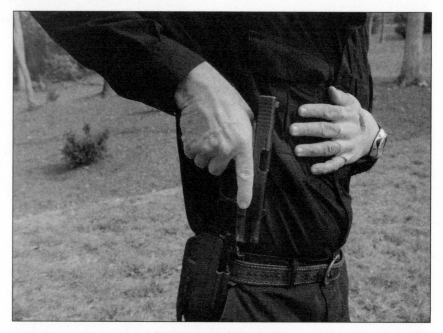

Remove weapon from holster

Let the slide go forward

Prepare to shoot from hip if required

Bring weapon to firing position

*Tap weapon
on knee*

*Rack, slide using
belt buckle or shoe*

*Remove the
magazine*

Holster the empty weapon

Reach for a new magazine

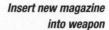

Insert new magazine into weapon

Remove weapon from holster

As you bring your weapon up, acquire a good firing grip. Remember to keep a straight finger until your sights are on the target and you have made the conscious decision to shoot.

It is very difficult to perform this technique quickly. Those who are ambidextrous and those who train regularly with each hand independently will have a definite advantage with these skills.

Every movement conducted with the support hand will be more awkward, slower, and less efficient. This is exactly why these skills must be practiced—despite the likelihood of ever actually needing to use any of the above skills being statistically remote.

Bring weapon to the ready position and prepare to fire if required

Using the rear sight, rack the slide to the rear to chamber a round

This training should not be overemphasized when compared to the basic fundamentals. As Chuck Taylor, a world class IPSC competitor, once said, "Do not spend disproportionate time and effort in weak-hand shooting when, in truth, it is rarely required. Therefore, no more than 10–15 percent of your practice time should be spent dealing with it."

Reach behind back and aquire grip

BASIC KNEELING POSITIONS

Kneeling positions are easy to assume for most people and provide the shooter with a stable platform. The kneeling position has the advantage of providing good mobility and presents a much smaller target. With the kneeling position, you can seek cover behind smaller objects allowing for increased stability and balance.

Author in unsupported kneeling position

Variations include:

- one knee—supported
- one knee—unsupported
- both knees—unsupported

These can be modified to include:

- resting on rear foot
- resting back on both feet
- muscle on bone (triceps, quadriceps, knee). But avoid bone on bone, e.g., elbow on knee, since this configuration can cause the shooting hand to wobble while

*Author shooting
from the kneeling
supported position*

Clockwise from left: Jon F. demonstrating the supported kneeling position; Jim C. demonstrating the use of various kneeling positions

shooting. You may find that supporting your shooting elbow with your quadriceps or the inside of your thigh works best. Or you may need to have your knee brace your upper arm to attain comfort, balance, and stability.

Training with our Asian allies

*Top: **Author** using available cover, behind vehicle, while shooting from prone position.*
*Right: **Jon F.** using available cover, in front of vehicle, while shooting from prone position.*

Behind Cover and/or Concealment:

- The ideal position is on the right knee if on the right side of the cover/concealment, and on the left knee if on the left side of the cover/concealment (you want your outside knee down to limit your exposure). However, if you end up on the wrong knee, go with it. Keeping your thigh (your femoral artery) behind cover is very important. A rupture of that artery can cause the shooter to bleed out and die within three to five minutes.

Author firing his long gun from the kneeling position

Author in the unsupported kneeling position

- As the knee hits the ground, the weapon should be extended fully, and you should be ready to shoot or scan.
- Do not crowd cover/concealment. You should be at least an arm's length away from the object concealing you. Cover/concealment can work from a good distance away. It's a matter of angles.
- Always keep the cover/concealment between you and the threat.

All body types are different and it probably will take a bit of experimentation to find which positions are most suitable for you.

Top: Author firing his long gun from the prone position, preparing to move to next firing position. Bottom: Author firing his AK with a bipod from the prone position.

The point is to practice the positions you feel comfortable with over and over again until they become instinctive.

Your shooting position may be determined by available cover, e.g., standing behind a telephone pole or lying prone behind a fallen tree. An ideal cover position should provide you with the best possible view of the threat and the best possible shot while providing adequate cover.

There are times when you may find yourself in an awkward and unnatural position. Imagine if you have to take a shot after being attacked in bed, or if you're sitting in a chair, or driving, or if you trip and fall. What if you fall after being shot? None of these positions are natural and it's unlikely that you will have spent much time preparing to take a shot from them. You have to be flexible, adaptable, and ready to shoot from almost any position.

Author in a prone position

Author moving into the prone Position

READY POSITIONS

"The object of shooting is hitting, and since the defensive shooter must hit quickly, the relationship between the ready position and the basic marksmanship fundamentals are evident."

—Jeff Cooper

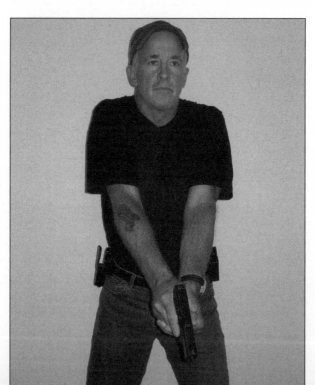

Low ready position

There is no better option than to have your weapon at the ready position before the shooting starts!

Tactical Ready

The tactical ready position must:

- Permit movement without compromising any advantage the shooter has.
- Place a minimal impact on the ability of the shooter to place quick, effective shots.
- Not allow the weapon to precede the shooter into an uncleared area or blind space.
- Lend itself to good muzzle control, a fundamental safety issue that can never be disregarded. In the heat of the moment it can be easy to forget about safety.

Author demonstrating "shooting while moving," concentrating on keeping a full field of vision while in motion.

- Allow the shooter the opportunity to retain the weapon in the case of the threat trying to take hold of it. Weapon retention is of vital importance.

Close Quarters Ready

- Is assumed with the weapon held close to the chest with the weapon to the midline of the body, and with the bore approximately where you would normally clap your hands. In this position the muzzle can be quickly moved in most directions with ease.
- A tactical ready position that facilitates a quick first shot while keeping the weapon back to minimize the possibility of a disarm.

Author in close quarters ready position

Not only is the weapon less accessible to a threat but, if someone tries to grab it, you can exert greater strength from this position than with the weapon extended.

- The muzzle is forward and the elbows drawn back until the wrists or forearms touch the chest. It is easy to maintain for long periods of time and the weapon is close to the body for protection.

- Depending on the situation, the muzzle can be oriented toward the threat, up, down, or toward the non-dominant side.
- Keep you trigger finger straight until you have made the conscious decision to shoot and your sights are on the threat.

The close quarters ready position does not project an aggressive posture to the same degree that pointing the weapon with extended arms does. In fact, as surprising as it may seem, in some instances the threat may not even see your weapon.

Do not discount body language as a significant factor in dominating a situation. If the distance between you and the threat allows, extending the weapon toward the threat not only projects aggressive body language but typically allows for a more effective shot.

Low Ready

The low ready position, with the muzzle down 45 degrees to the target, may keep you from inadvertently pointing it at someone who suddenly happens to emerge in front of you.

Author in low ready position

Sul Ready

If you want your weapon drawn but do not want to appear "too threatening," consider the "sul," or "south," position. This position requires that you break your firing grip altogether and point the muzzle straight down. The tips of your two thumbs index against each other, and your dominant hand's middle finger indexes against the nondominant index finger.

You can quickly shift to close quarters ready as the situation permits.

"Sul" or south ready position

The "sul" position allows you to move very near to other people without pointing your weapon at them. From a safety standpoint it's almost as safe as having the weapon holstered provided the muzzle is pointed straight down and not covering any body parts.

Whenever a weapon is drawn keep it out in front of you and in a safe direction where you can always see it. If you can't see your own weapon, you are not in control of it. During training, utilize your index points, e.g., elbows indexed to your rib cage, grip in touch with each index point, so that your ready positions become incorporated into your subconscious.

THE DRAW STROKES

"It's not how fast you move, it's how soon you get there ready to shoot."
—Rob Leatham

Although the draw is not a marksmanship fundamental it is included here since it is an essential step that is typically taken before getting into a ready position. The draw should be practiced while standing, kneeling, sitting, prone, or any awkward shooting positions you may find yourself in after falling, getting shot, injured, etc. If at all possible, it is always better to draw first before moving into any position from the standing position. It should also be noted that a quick draw is no substitute for good awareness skills.

The most efficient way to bring your weapon to the firing position is straight out, bringing the sights up to eye level.

As you punch the weapon straight out, do not add any unnecessary movements. Some shooters tend to add in a bowler's technique to their method and others add in the fisherman's cast technique. Both of these added movements take the sights off of the target and waste valuable time.

Your arms do not have to be out to full extension. Punch out to just short of full extension. This will reduce the amount of muscular and tendon tension.

One of the most common errors made is when the shooter punches out too forcefully, causing the weapon muzzle to dip at full or close to full arm extension. The wrist will tend to flex at full extension if done too forcefully and the shooter will shoot low.

Ready position

Defensive Strong-Side Draw

The defensive strong-side draw allows the shooter to draw the weapon quickly, consistently, and safely and facilitates a response to both contact-distance threats and those at longer range.

Both hands moving at the same time. Support hand at center of chest.

Acquire a good shooting grip

Pull the weapon to clear the holster

Pivot the weapon toward the threat

Acquire a good two-handed grip maintaining a straight shooting finger until your sights are on the target and you have made the decision to shoot.

Weapon up to near full extension

Prepare to shoot

Look over weapon for other threats

Scan left and right

Check 360 degrees before holstering

The defensive draw stroke occurs in two phases: acceleration and deceleration. All of the below draw steps should be executed while your eyes are on the target/threat or scanning the area for threats— not looking down at your holster.

Acceleration Phase

- Move both hands at the same time. The support hand moves to the midline while the shooting hand moves to the grip.
- Move the shooting hand down on the pistol from the top to establish a good firing grip.
- Move laterally off the line of attack and to cover if available, simultaneously with the first step of the draw stroke. You can literally dodge a bullet with this movement.

Concealed, strong side draw

- As you step off the attack line, lean forward to shift your weight toward the threat into the modified isosceles stance. This puts you in your shooting stance as quickly as possible and also braces you against a possible charging threat.
- If a thumb break is required, the pad of the thumb indexes on the thumb break, and releases it at a 45-degree angle toward the body.

- If a concealment garment is worn, clear it as the shooting hand moves to the pistol. With an unbuttoned coat, jacket, or shirt, claw the garment back with all fingers on the shooting hand. With a sweatshirt, buttoned shirt, or similar attire, pull it high with both hands, initially grabbing the bottom of the shirt as near the holster as possible. You may also want to lean away from the holster at this time since it will allow the garment to clear more easily.

• As the garment is cleared and the weapon is gripped, move the support hand to the chest, thumb pointed up along the center-line of the body—your "clapping position." This puts the support hand in position to assume a two-handed high grip on the weapon and stages it to execute hand-to-hand combat techniques if required. In a contact-distance situation, the support hand can hit the threat at the neck or above with a hand/arm blow or block an edged weapon attack. In response to a sudden assault, the support hand may perform one of these actions in lieu of moving to the center of the chest.

- The pads of the middle two fingers are indexed under the grip.
- The shooting-side elbow remains above the hand and not out to the side of the hand.
- The web of the shooting hand makes contact high on the grip and under the tang.
- When you draw the weapon from its holster, make sure that your finger does not enter the trigger guard until your sights are on target and you have made the conscious decision to shoot (Safety Rule #3).
- The weapon is removed from the holster with the middle two fingers by "popping it" out of the holster.

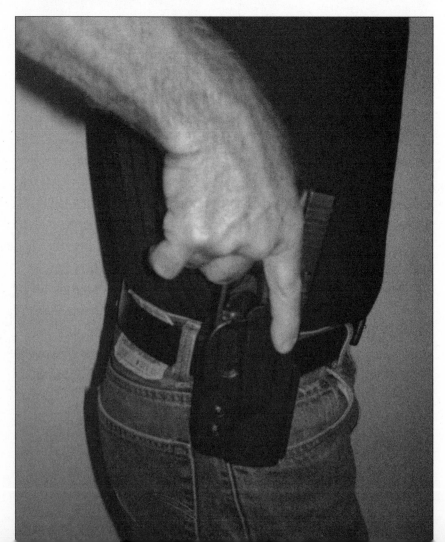

- As the weapon clears the holster, rotate the muzzle forward, putting the hand, wrist, and arm in their final alignment. The shooting-side elbow should stay close to the body; avoid letting it "chicken wing" to the side.
- The barrel and muzzle remain parallel to the ground.
- When dealing with a threat at contact distance, you may elect to remain in the weapon retention position until you can create good reactive distance. Depending on the circumstances, you can shoot, use the gun as an impact weapon or cover the threat. A close range confrontation may require any of these actions, so remain flexible.
- These initial movements should be performed as quickly as possible. Accelerate 0–90.

Deceleration Phase

- As you bring the weapon to bear, decelerate smoothly, 90–0. If you continue at full speed to the end of your draw stroke, the weapon will come to a jarring halt, which will produce unwanted vibrations, like a tuning fork, that will require you to have to wait before you shoot.
- Place the weapon lightly on target, like ringing a door bell.
- The sooner you move the weapon to your sight line, the sooner you can start using the sights to refine and confirm weapon alignment.
- Think of *pulling* the weapon forward to the desired spot with your fingers rather than pushing it with the palms of your hands. Mentally project the front sight onto the target as you bring the weapon up.
- Think of how easy it would be to hit the target if the front sight were actually touching it; visualizing the sight there accomplishes much the same thing in your mind.
- The weapon is brought up to the "ready" position as soon as the muzzle extends beyond the support hand and the hands come

together. If the weapon has an external safety, it can be taken off safe at this time.

- The weapon travels from your body's centerline up to the centerline of the target/threat.
- Alternatively, extend the weapon with one hand unsupported. In either case, the muzzle should track vertically up the threat's centerline.
- Bring the sights up to your eyes, rather than your eyes down to your sights.
- Move the trigger finger to the trigger only after the sights are on target/threat and you have made the conscious decision to shoot.
- Once you have made the conscious decision to shoot, prep the trigger by taking the slack out as you extend your arms. Apply the final pressure to the trigger just as the weapon comes to a complete halt, verifying weapon alignment via the sights or other feedback as the weapon comes to a stop, when possible. After the shot, reset and prep the trigger for the next shot.
- You can stop this process halfway to deal with a contact-distance threat.

Defensive Strong-Side Holster

- To holster simply perform the same steps but in reverse order.
- The weapon comes straight back so the base of the thumb makes contact with the side of the pectoral muscle. At this point, you simply pivot your weapon so the barrel is pointing down, but not at your feet.
- Ride your thumb down your ribs with the muzzle pointing directly downward, and reseat the weapon into the holster.
- Position your thumb over the back of the slide to prevent the weapon from "coming out of battery" when holstering for a Semi-automatic. For revolvers keep the base of the thumb in contact

with your ribs all the way down your side until the muzzle is in the holster. This will prevent you from "lasering" yourself.

- Keep the trigger finger extended straight when holstering. This not only helps point the weapon into the holster, but guarantees the finger will not catch between trigger and holster.
- By keeping your thumb on the rear of the slide and your trigger finger extended, you can prevent an accidental discharge from occurring.

Have another qualified shooter observe your draw stroke and holster stroke to ensure the muzzle does not sweep any part of your body while drawing or holstering. This is especially important when drawing from a seated position, as when in a vehicle or while sitting at a table. You'll need to modify this procedure for use with shoulder holsters, fanny packs, ankle rigs, etc.

Cross Draw

Use your support hand to sweep clothing away. After you acquire a good grip on the weapon, move the support hand out of the way, to avoid sweeping yourself. Come to the ready position and then come "up" to scan or shoot using the techniques described above.

Close Quarters Draw

Weapon retention and warding off any threat while drawing is always paramount. Use your support arm to block or to redirect the threat's attack. Try to blade your body from the threat by taking a step back with your strong foot. Most of your weight should be on this strong foot. At the same time, your dominant hand reaches for the weapon and your support hand lifts to guard from the attack. Lean away from the target. You will end up looking underneath the raised support hand. Be sure to keep the support hand clear from the weapon. Come to the ready position and "up," to scan or to shoot.

Within Arms Reach (WAR) assault

Speed Rock

The speed rock has been taught to shooters since the early 1900s. It involves leaning back at the waist and firing your weapon just as it clears and pivots from your holster. This draw stroke is intended only for those situations where there is no other alternative, for instance if you are grabbed or pushed over the hood of a car. It is best used if the threat is right on top of you. This technique does not work well if your back is up against the wall you since you will not be able to draw.

Keep your dominant wrist tight against the body, just under the pectoral muscle. If the wrist comes off the body, it becomes easier for an assailant to take the weapon. Point the weapon slightly outward to allow the hammer and/or slide to clear your body and clothing, and also because with so little clearance of the holster you can easily shoot yourself in the stomach.

Shoot as fast as you can pull the trigger until you can break contact with the threat and try to gain some reactive distance. You can then finish the fight with visually verified fire if need be.

The speed rock is very fast, and denies the threat access to your weapon. But, this technique puts you severely off balance in order to raise the bullet point of impact to the threat's upper chest. You may need to consider shooting the threat's pelvis as an option given that center mass shots are difficult for some shooters and may only reach the stomach.

Step Back/Shove 'n' Shoot

This step back technique is instinctive. Strike the threat in the chest or face (usually with a palm-heel strike), then take one to several steps back or to the side, draw, and shoot. It requires defenders to move backward into an area they can't see. In many cases taking a single shuffle step backward or at an angle will not present a danger, since what's in that space is probably something the defender is aware of.

Essentially, since you can't move backward as quickly as your attacker can move forward, you are depending on your strike to disable or disorient him long enough for you to draw.

Drive Forward

This technique will appeal to those with martial arts experience. Instead of deflecting the attack or moving back, you use your non-dominant arm to strike or drive into the threat while simultaneously drawing your weapon and shooting.

This technique adheres to the fundamental principles of conflict by employing what is always the most effective defense—a strong offense. It does not require the defender to move into unknown space, and it will probably greatly surprise the threat, turning the threat's advantage to the defender.

This draw stroke requires some strength, and it may not be instinctive for all shooters to aggressively move into their attacker. Also, if you meet resistance to your counteroffensive, you can easily find yourself in a hand-to-hand fight instead.

The effectiveness of this technique is directly proportional to the unarmed skill level of the defender.

Drop to Deck

This technique involves dropping to the deck onto your back or either side, and folding your legs, keeping all four limbs off the ground and fighting from there.

This is a complicated technique, involving multiple difficult skills: falling correctly, keeping your limbs off the ground, and ground fighting. Once you're on the ground, you'll probably be there without other options until the conflict is over.

Being on the ground puts you at a considerable disadvantage as it is difficult to draw, shoot and fight from this position. However, if you fall or are pushed down, you're going to have to fight and shoot from the ground, so you should know how to do it correctly. If there is no other escape route from a close-in assault, this may be your only option.

Run!

As a last resort, and depending upon the circumstances, you may need to turn and run to cover as fast as possible, then draw and shoot. You would need to run for at least 15 yards to significantly lessen the chances of being shot.

Common Errors During the Draw

- Looking down at the holster and weapon and not keeping your eyes on the target/threat.
- Fumbling for the weapon because it is not where you expect it to be or you are not used to carrying the weapon.
- Not indexing properly on the thumb snap and front strap before drawing.
- Not allowing the web of the hand to contact the weapon first.
- Shooting with your elbow excessively flared out to the side.

- Not straightening the strong wrist into the firing angle after clearing the holster.
- Not controlling the attitude of the weapon as it comes up to the target.
- Not punching straight out with the weapon, either by dipping (bowling technique) or flipping (fishing technique).
- Punching out too forcibly rather than like "ringing the door bell."
- Putting your finger on the trigger too early and beginning to press the trigger too early.
- Sweeping your support hand or any part of your body.

To Holster

Before holstering you should have assessed the condition of known threats' follow-through; scanned for additional threats; reloaded; and moved to cover as appropriate.

Regardless of the draw stroke you use, simply work backwards one step at a time, to the two-handed close quarters ready position described above, then to the point that the hands separate from the pistol, and ultimately to the holster.

If you fire from a low shooting position, e.g., prone, kneeling, squatting, or sitting, and it's appropriate to the tactical situation, stand and scan before holstering. This will allow you to see more of the area and will help to prevent you from pointing the weapon at your legs.

Perform a final 360-degree scan, then holster and refasten any retention devices.

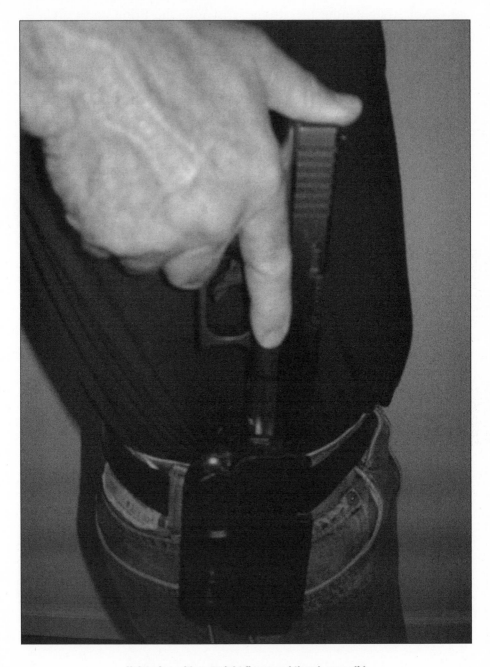

Holstering with a straight finger and thumb over slide

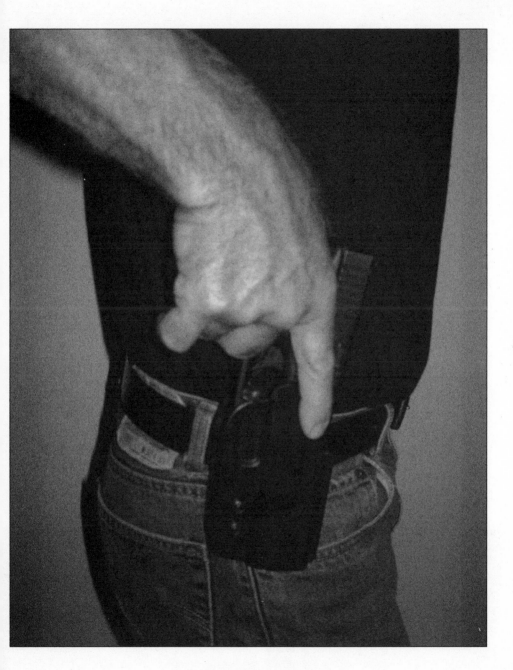

Drawing with a straight finger.

GRIP AND TRIGGER CONTROL

The Grip

When holding a pistol, you want the web of the hand to be on the back of the grip as close to the tang (the projection where the grip meets the frame) as possible. This moves the bore axis lower into your hand and reduces the leverage that the weapon has to raise its muzzle in recoil. The middle fingers wrap around the grip and the

One of the most critical fundamentals is a proper shooting grip

forefinger (trigger finger) lies straight along the barrel. If you leave a space between the web of the hand and the tang of the grip, the muzzle will "flip" higher in recoil. If that gap is closed, your hand gains greater leverage for better control.

Place the dominant hand thumb high, relatively parallel to the bore so a space is left for the optimal placement of the non-dominant hand and thumb.

The idea is to already be in a shooting grip when you pivot the weapon out of the holster and into a firing position. The more naturally this occurs, the faster you can actually be ready to shoot.

When selecting a weapon, consider the grip size and the grip-to-bore angle. The closer the grip angle is to 90 degrees the more the muzzle will dip if the weapon is punched out too hard. Handguns with greater grip-to-barrel angles point more naturally and are less susceptible to muzzle dip.

When purchasing a weapon, take your time and try out different weapons with different grip angles. When possible, ask if you can fire the weapon before you purchase it.

- The pistol grip is of critical importance and acquiring it quickly and properly takes quite a bit of training. The handgun should be gripped with the bore of the weapon in line with the forearm. This allows the barrel to act as a natural extension of the arm, which helps control recoil and weapon retention.
- Grip tension must remain constant once the grip is set. Grip tension should be approximately that of a good firm handshake. Once you have acquired your good grip, all that should move is that isolated trigger finger—nothing else.

   Note: Many professional shooters use a grip ratio of 60:40. The support hand provides 60 percent of the grip strength and the shooting hand provides 40 percent of the grip strength. This prevents the shooting finger from being too stressed when squeezing back on the trigger.

Increasing friction and reducing leverage are two of the main priorities in establishing a good grip.

- Friction: Increase the surface area of the weapon as much as possible with both your dominant hand and your nondominant hand. Friction tape or grip wraps properly placed on the grip can

enhance the amount of friction and can be used as additional index points.

- Leverage: Reduce the leverage of the weapon by holding it high up on the tang, as close to the axis of recoil as possible. A good analogy would be to hold the weapon as though you were holding a snake high up on its head so that it cannot bite you. The web of the hand should be as high as possible to keep the bore in line with the arm horizontally and to reduce muzzle rise during firing.

Duane Thomas, a writer for *Guns & Ammo,* states that "No one knows more about fast and accurate handgunning than the USPSA/

"It's all in the hands. The hands are the part of the body that interact most directly with a handgun. And how the gun reacts to its own recoil depends on how the shooter grips it.

Ideally, what we want is a grip technique that causes the gun to point naturally at the target; we shouldn't have to waste any time searching for and aligning the sights. Also, when the gun fires, we want it to track consistently, e.g. return to the exact same spot with no effort on our part. If we make that happen and learn how to reset the trigger action while the gun is still in recoil (an entirely different topic), we can fire the gun as fast as it comes down out of recoil and still be accurate."
—Brian Enos

IPSC Grand Masters. These guys are the gods of high-speed precision handgunning. Even among Grand Masters there are Grand Masters, Brian Enos and Rob Leatham". Brian and Rob developed the straight-thumbs method of gripping a handgun that is the standard among serious shooters today.

Brian Enos's career as a sponsored shooter spanned over two decades, with Smith & Wesson, European American Armory, and Strayer-Voigt. He went 1–2 with Robbie Leatham at the 1983 Nationals; won the Bianchi Cup back-to-back in '83–'84 and the Masters in '89; and in the '90s was a member of the winning three-man Sportsman's Team Challenge team five times. He wrote *Prac-*

tical Shooting: Beyond Fundamentals, the most useful shooting manual in the history of IPSC. In 2000 he started www.brianenos .com, a very successful Internet Web site and pro shop.

Revolver Grip

The revolver grip is slightly different than the grip used with a semi. The thumb of the shooting hand is tucked down on the grip and the support hand thumb is placed over the shooting hand thumb. Double-action revolvers are fired more efficiently if the dominant-hand thumb is bent downward to "lock" into the middle finger.

The Wrist

The wrist is the most influential joint and one of the most important elements of a good shooting position. It's the most versatile tool at your disposal. It gives you the ability to rotate the weapon with ease, and it greatly affects your trigger finger.

Brian Enos acquiring a good grip

If the sight picture is adjusted by movement in the wrist, the wrist still tends to go back to its strongest position as the shot is fired, an instinct that helps combat recoil. For this reason, the handgun should be grasped firmly, stabilizing the wrist in its strongest position. Adjustments in sight picture should be made by the position of the feet and motion at the other joints, such as ankles, knees, and shoulders.

Trigger Control

I am not worried about the threat that can bench press 400 pounds. I realize there are many threats much stronger than I can ever hope to be. But I also know that with just a few pounds of pressure and proper shot placement I can neutralize any threat out there.

Proper trigger control allows the shooter to fire a shot without disturbing the sight picture. The trigger must be pressed smoothly to the rear, without any disturbance of the sight picture, until the pressure suffices and the weapon discharges. As a matter of fact, you could be the very best marksman in the world if your never disturbed your

sight picture when you pulled the trigger. Obviously, this is much easier said than done.

Hold your body as still as possible while tracking the front sight through the recoil cycle, and relax. This will allow the firing pin platform to be still until the round has left the barrel and keeps the pistol within the target area in the event another shot is required.

Two key elements to this are finger placement and the "surprise break."

Some shooters tend to push or pull the trigger to the side rather than pulling it straight back. Many shooters also tend to flinch—and since they are anticipating the shot going off, they shoot low or "jerk the weapon." It is almost as if someone were to ask you to look at an M-80 firecracker as it goes off two feet in front of your face: Just before you see the fuse disappear, you are bound to flinch before it explodes. This is the flinch that you must get rid of.

A simple dry fire exercise involves placing a piece of brass at the far end of the muzzle and pulling the trigger. You should be able to do this without the brass falling off the weapon.

Trigger Finger

It's imperative that you learn to isolate your trigger finger. In order to shoot multiple shots accurately and quickly, you must control direction, speed, and effort. Shooting should be almost rhythmic.

Only allow the trigger finger to move. Be sure that the other parts of your hand do not move when pressing the trigger back. The faster you press the trigger the greater the chance your other fingers and your hand will adversely affect your trigger control.

With many semiautomatics, your trigger finger should be placed on the middle of the trigger with the middle of the pad of the finger as you press back. Do not allow the second joint of the trigger finger to move while moving the pad back and forth.

Police training off-hand shooting

Depending on the type of trigger and the amount of pressure it requires to fire the weapon, the finger placement should allow you to press straight to the rear without any lateral movement. Placing too much of the finger, or conversely, not placing enough finger on the trigger, will cause your shots to string laterally on the target.

Some triggers are easier to operate than others, but all can be managed with proper training. With the Glock (which the ATF has classified the safe-action trigger systems as double action only) or the single-action triggers the area of the middle of the first pad of the finger seems to work best for most shooters. If your weapon is a double-action or revolver it will require more finger on the trigger in order to provide the leverage necessary to compress the heavier trigger. For these shooters the area just above the first joint works better.

Single-and Double-Action Trigger

On the single-action weapons like the Glock, there is slack in the trigger which allows for a safety margin prior to firing.

More advanced shooters often will take up the slack, or "prep the trigger," to the point where the hammer or the firing pin is about to be released. This is a somewhat controversial technique, but effective when done right. Press using constant speed, effort, and controlled direction.

After firing, release the trigger just past the point where it resets and prep it again if you are going to fire another shot. It is definitely worthwhile to practice trigger reset drills during dry fire. This can be done by having a buddy stand beside you when you dry fire. After you press the trigger back and the dry shot fires, he can rack the slide back before you reset the trigger, allowing you to feel and hear the trigger reset.

With a double-action trigger, maintain steady pressure all the way through the pull phase. In slow fire shooting and/or precision shooting, staging the trigger is a common practice. This involves pressing the trigger to the point where the firing pin or hammer is about to be released and then stopping and adjusting the sight picture before the trigger is slowly pressed the rest of the way.

The Surprise Break

A surprise break occurs when the shooter applies smooth and steady pressure until eventually and almost unintentionally, the pressure is sufficient to "break" the trigger.

Align the sights on target and establish a sight picture. Next, focus visually on the front sight while building smooth and steady pressure on the trigger until eventually the weapon fires.

A shooter should never anticipate the "break" of the trigger. He knows that it is going to go, and is continually applying constant pressure on the trigger, but does not know the precise instant when it will "break." The trigger must break almost unintentionally. If the shooter anticipates the break, or forces it to occur, he will invariably bear down reflexively on the weapon and flinch at the final moment (jerk the trigger), which often causes the shot to go low.

Just as the human eye can focus only on one specific thing at a time, the human mind operates in much the same way. If you mentally focus your attention on the front sight as you press the trigger straight back and do not anticipate the shot going off, you will have a "surprise break." This concept is often difficult to teach since most people wonder how they cannot anticipate a shot that they know is going to happen.

Through proper training, perfect practice, and repetition you will be able to control the trigger in the same way as with the surprise break, and in less time. This is called the "compressed" surprise break.

In a combat situation, you will most likely not have the amount of time you'd like to get the sights on target and press the trigger. In order to maintain trigger control you must hold your body as still as the circumstances allow while pressing the trigger. Accept the recoil and don't try to fight it or react to it.

Overt and Covert Indexes

Indexing makes practicing perfect practice all the easier. The reference points that you use when indexing will greatly increase the likelihood that you will do every step the same exact way, each and every time.

The key is to try to always carry out each movement in the way that has proven to be the most efficient, safest, and quickest for you. If every time you shoot your stance is different or your grip is different, etc., you will never perfect your shooting techniques.

With weapons training, use as many reference index points as possible and practice to ensure your stance, grip, etc. are exactly the same. For example, when in the ready position, my elbows are indexed against my rib cage; my straight finger, with my shooting hand, is alongside the frame; my thumb is on the slide stop; and the web of my hand is up high on the tang. Every weapon you operate will have its own index points.

You will want to index your grip the same way every time you're drawing and holding your weapon. Get a good feel of your weapon(s). If you are using an unfamiliar weapon, place it in your hands and learn the indexes you will use.

When carrying a concealed weapon, "covert index" using your elbows or forearms to ensure your weapon and magazines are where they need to be. If someone were to try to grab your weapon, you would have a better chance of at least blocking that person. In the case of a threat—say, you just shifted from condition yellow to orange, but have not yet made the decision to draw—you should at least index your weapon.

It is also important to index your magazines for quick reloads. For instance, your straight support index finger should be down the side of the magazine.

Be sure to always wear your holster and magazine pouch in the exact location. If you do not, it will be more difficult to index your weapon and magazines the same way every time.

• Overt Index: Place your shooting hand on the grip and be ready to draw and deal with the threat(s). If your weapon is concealed, you can prep your butt pack, or reach inside your shirt/jacket and index the weapon.

- Covert Index: When in Condition Orange you may want to place the inside of your forearm against the grip of the weapon. This is for both concealed and open carry. Your mind is now actively thinking about the next possible step—to draw and take whatever action is required.

COMMON ERRORS IN TRIGGER MANIPULATION

- Failure to isolate the trigger finger. As the speed increases, so does the tendency to involve the other fingers or hand.
- Rocking the pad of the finger across the face of the trigger, which can push or pull the trigger sideways instead of keeping steady pressure across the face of the trigger.
- Staging the trigger with a subsequent flinch at the end of the press. Pressing should be one steady motion. (According to Ron Avery, whose methodology is currently being used by different government agencies and thousands of individuals across the United States and internationally, shooters can practice avoiding this error by slowly saying the word "squeeze" as they press the trigger.)
- Not controlling the duration of the trigger press and pushing or pulling the weapon to the side.

VISUAL TECHNIQUES AND SIGHT ALIGNMENT

Vision

Our vision is our most important sense. Our eyes do far more than give us a picture of the environment. They coordinate with various skeletal muscles to assist with balance and movement, and by the "stereoscopic effect"—wherein two eyes a fixed distance apart see things from slightly different angles—they provide us with depth perception.

Closing the nondominant eye. in order to focus through sights reduces the ability of the eyes to perform these other functions. However, for longer shots, it is sometimes better to partially close the nondominant eye to get rid of the double vision effect. Every shooter has to determine what works best for him.

Training Tip: Do not become distracted when shooting. Avoid stress anxiety. Imagine how you want to shoot, visualize your movements, your steps and your procedures: "I will be calm, everything will be perfect."

In closer situations, there is a definite advantage to keeping both eyes open, since less dependence is placed on the sights and more on the threat or the area of concern.

Fortunately, the eye is incredibly fast, and able to change focal distances in hundredths of a second. It takes practice, but over time a shooter can learn to focus alternately on the sights and the target so quickly (eye sprints) that it seems simultaneous. To practice this all you need to do is to point at a distant object then line up your dominant eye with your finger and the object. Close your non-dominant eye. Now, quickly shift your focal length so the first object is sharply in focus, then your finger. Repeat at least 8–10 times or so for each practice session. Try the same exercise with your non-dominant eye. And like everything else, the more practice, the easier it gets and the quicker you will be.

Another good reason to practice shooting with both eyes open is that when a person is attacked or feels threatened, his eyes open wide and his eyebrows lift to allow for a wider and greater field of vision. This is an involuntary reflex. Fighting against it to close an eye for focus can delay your readiness to shoot. Try opening both eyes wide then closing just one of them. It is unnatural and takes longer to focus.

Sight Alignment

Sight alignment is the relationship between the front sight, the rear sight, and the shooter's eye(s). The "focal continuum" is defined as the number of infinite focal points between the target and the eye. Unfortunately, the eye can only focus on one focal point at a time. Other points on the focal continuum become out of focus and blurry.

Sight alignment is established by placing your visual focus on the front sight and aligning it with the rear sight. This is the objective if you have the time to place a well-aimed shot. The top of the front sight must be seen as level with the top of the rear sight. Additionally, you must see equal amounts of space visible on both sides of the front sight as viewed through the rear sight. This describes perfect vertical and horizontal alignment of the sights.

Oftentimes we have to settle for less if the threat is close. The greater the distance to the target, the more important it is to use the sights. The closer the target is, the bigger it appears, and the less perfect your sight alignment needs to be.

You need to be 100 percent in favor of "gun control." Achieve it through proper stance, proper sight alignments, proper grip, smooth trigger control, and follow-through.

> "During practice, become aware of exactly how and when you see your sights. Do you see them silhouetted like a giant building on the skyline, or maybe you don't remember any details of the sights themselves. (Don't think of good and bad, just see what you see.) As the gun is moving toward the target, when do you 'pick up' the sights? Do you see them as they are approaching the target, as they touch the target, or after the gun is stopped on the target? As the shot is firing, do you see the sights lift up, or are you looking for the next target? How does this vary according to the types and placement of the targets?"
>
> —Brian Enos

Front Sight Focus

Human beings are only capable of focusing on a single object at a time. First look at the target or individual to determine if it is a threat. Often this can only be done by looking at what the target/individual is holding in his hands. Keep both eyes open. This point needs to

Training Tip: The classic "double tap" has potentially deadly consequences, if the double tap or controlled pair is not enough.

be stressed because many newer shooters will try to ID the target or scan an area by looking through the sights, which is very difficult to do—like "looking at the world through a straw." If you determine you are facing a threat because the person is either holding a weapon and/or placing your life in jeopardy and has an opportunity to impose grave bodily harm on you, then you must react quickly—as though your life depends on it.

After you have identified a threat, bring your eyes to center mass, the head, or the pelvis. If time and distance allow your eyes should then focus away from the threat and to the sights. At this point you are actually looking at the threat, the front sight, and the rear sight. Focus on the front sight. The target and the rear sight should appear out of focus and the front sight will be crisp, clear, and in sharp focus. When you squeeze the trigger, do not disturb this sight picture and you will shoot exactly where you are aiming.

Many novice shooters find it difficult to focus on the front sight. If you do not have the luxury of reactive time or distance you may simply look over the sights or you may just point and shoot. These options will be discussed later in the book.

Sight Picture

Sight picture is defined as the existing sight alignment as it appears superimposed on the target. Since the human eye is similar to a camera, in that it can only focus on one item at a time, careful attention must be given to focusing on the front sight. In precision shooting the focus is always on the front sight. If you looked at the target, front sight, and rear sight through a camera and focused the lens on the front sight, you would still see the target and the rear site but they would be out of focus when compared to the front sight.

The more difficult the shot (e.g. distance, size of target, light conditions, etc.), the more precise that sight picture must be. Visual and mental focus must remain on the front sight before squeezing off the shot. The sights are not going to remain absolutely still while sighting. This leads many novice shooters to jerk the shot when they think that they've got the perfect sight picture. Jerking the shot, however, usually results in a hit that's low and to the non-dominant side, as the result of poor trigger control.

Increase the pressure on the trigger as the sights wobble and let the weapon go off somewhat unexpectedly. Shots can typically be kept within an eight-inch group—"combat accuracy " if you're no more than seven yards away, as long as the front sight appears somewhere inside the notch of the rear sight. This becomes increasingly difficult the further away you are from your target.

Most shooters have no problem at all keeping both eyes open up to 10 or so feet and some shooters can keep both eyes open out to 20 feet. This is based on the individual and every shooter has to experiment to see just how far they can be from a target with both eyes open, as well as with the non-dominant eye partially closed or the non-dominant eye fully closed.

For most shooters their dominant eye is the same as the dominant hand. So, most right-handed shooters are right-eye dominant, but that is not always the case. Some shooters are cross-eyed dominant, e.g., right-handed shooter, left-eye dominant or vice versa. It is important to know, without doubt, which is your dominant eye. There are a number of ways you can check to see which eye is dominant.

Bring both hands out at arm's length and make a triangle with your hands. Look at an object through this small triangle. Now bring your hands directly to your eyes. It should go directly over your dominant eye.

So, when you need to close one eye and your primary-side eye is dominant, simply partially close or close the support-side eye while focusing on the front sight. If your dominant eye is on the support side, you have options. Either focus with the non-dominant eye, or close that non-dominant eye and modify your head by angling it to allow the support-side eye access to the sights.

Keeping both eyes open is the preferred method if one can focus on the front sight. But this is not always the reality. It is true that most gunfights happen within three meters, but even with that understood, it may be dark, the threat may be behind cover, or you may be in a bad shooting position and/or wounded. It is okay to close an eye for a split second or so in order to get that accurate shot. The non-dominant eye will only be closed while the shots are being fired. And after you fire always follow-through, ensuring the threat has been neutralized before scanning for other emerging threats. In the case of multiple threats, you may elect to scan prior to follow-through. This will be discussed later on in the book. In any event, you will not lose anything in your peripheral vision if you have to close your non-dominant eye for a split second or so. It is important you shoot what you intend to shoot and take an accurate shot.

Soft and Hard Focus

At closer ranges and at larger targets we use what is called a soft focus. Sometimes, depending on the distance and threat, we will simply look directly over the sights. The eyes may or may not even see the sights. They will see and focus on the target or an area between the target and the front sight. An analogy to describe this would be if you were driving down the road at 90 miles an hour and a tractor trailer pulled in front of you, would you be able to take your eye off the truck and focus on the small spot on your windshield? In other words, if the threat is big and dangerously close, your eyes will most likely remain on that threat and not shift to the sights. A hard focus would be focusing on the small spot on the windshield.

As mentioned earlier, different situations will require different levels of speed and accuracy. Larger and closer targets allow for faster shooting. Sight alignment and sight picture is not the same with the larger and closer targets as it is for the longer or more precise shot.

Your arm and body position, grip, and experience will all be factors in your having the ability to point and hit a large target in close proximity. Though the exact point of the hit may not be a perfect shot, two or three shots, with combat accuracy, will produce the desired results.

Many post shooting reports are similar to this one: "I didn't even see my sights or the threat, all I saw was his weapon. I do not know how many times I shot, I just kept firing until he went down."

The amount of focus, or focal shift, required is dependent upon the following factors:

- Your level of training and experience
- Your skill level
- Your distance from the threat
- The size of the threat
- The light (shadows, low light or no light)
- The ability of the eyes to focus on the threat

Ron Avery, one of the top shooters in the world, sums up the importance of sight alignment this way: "A critical element of shooting is to see what you need to see in terms of sight alignment and sight picture to make the hit." At closer distances, on bigger target areas, you can keep the sights basically aligned and fire the instant the front sight pauses in the impact area, he explains. As the demand for precision increases sight alignment and sight picture become more critical. The relationship between the top edge of the front sight and the target must be seen very clearly. This means that the vision will shift back to the front sight as the requirement for precision increases. During this process you're using your entire visual field to assist you.

Eye Dominance

As mentioned above the dominant eye provides most of the visual input to the brain. Some shooters have difficulty when their dominant eye is not the same as their dominant arm. A right-handed shooter with a left-dominant eye, for instance, may find it difficult to line up the sights. With a handgun, this problem is not so pronounced, as the sights are closer together and the rear sight is further from the eye than with a rifle. Either eye can be brought to focus on the sights with just about equal ease.

The best solution is to learn to shoot both left-handed and right-handed with equal ability. I know this sounds difficult, but it's actually not that challenging and it has the added advantage of allowing for better cover, since you will not have to expose as much of your body to shoot. For example, picture yourself shooting around the left corner of a building in a right-handed stance versus a left-handed stance.

And being able to shoot with your non-dominant hand, in this case, provides for much better balance than just shifting shoulders.

*Author shooting behind right side cover, on his right knee,
being careful not to expose any part of his body.*

No one wants or, for the most part, plans to be involved in a shooting. Most happen within seconds, leaving little time to evaluate the situation and to make decisions. In particular, shootings involving a handgun usually happen in close proximity and very quickly. Law enforcement refers to the "Rule of Threes"—three Meters, three Seconds, three Shots. The majority of law enforcement shootings fall into this category, or very near to it.

The FBI's "Law Enforcement Officers Killed and Assaulted Report," 1992, provides a detailed account of the law enforcement officers killed on duty over a ten-year period. During this time, the report covered 500 officers who were killed by handguns, 94 by rifles, and 56 with shotguns. A vast majority of the officers—365—were shot at ranges of 5 feet or less, or "conversational distance." Another 127 were killed at 6–10 feet, 77 were killed between 11–20 feet, and 79 were killed at 20 feet or more. These stats have not changed much over the years of documenting handgun shootings of law enforcement officers, meaning there is an 88 pecent chance that a law enforcement officer who is shot in the line of duty will be shot at 20 feet or less.

In this kind of close range scenario, a defensive shooter probably won't be paying any attention to the weapon sights. The target is right there, and the weapon simply becomes an extension of the hand, pointing as a finger would point.

At close range, keep your weapon close to your body, so it cannot be taken from you. Be careful not to obstruct your own vision by holding the weapon in front of your face. As the distance to the target increases, hold the weapon far enough from your body to use the sights, but no farther. Coordination decreases as your arm extends.

As the distance grows past 3 meters, a shooter needs to shift his focus more to the sights. From about 3–8 meters, the gun should be held high enough and out far enough to get a quick read through the sights to the target. How precise the read is depends on a number of factors, most importantly, how much time is available. Without some sighting, the chance of a miss or an ineffective shot increases significantly at these distances. A "hard focus" on the sights with the target being out of focus—but clear enough for the shot—is required at these distances.

When you are shooting at distances greater than about 8 meters, sighting becomes critical and a hard focus is required. Unsighted shooting beyond roughly 8 meters reduces the chances of a significant hit, especially if you and or the target is moving. A shooter needs a hard, concentrated focus on both the sights and the target, shifting between them in fractions of a second, to achieve an effective shot.

Point of Focus

Despite the fact that a person can have a wide field of vision, the human eye can only focus on a small area at any given time. This is because light rays must come into the lens of the eye from nearly the same angle—a "point of focus"—in order for the lens to focus at the "focal point."

You have to be able to shift quickly between various points of focus—the target, the target's hands, the sights, and the surrounding terrain. First, of course, is the potential threat. Does he have a weapon in his hands? If so, he may be a threat—or he may be your partner or family member. Depending on the distance, this is the time to align the sights on the target by bringing the visual focus to the front sight, as seen through the rear sight, and align the two points of reference on the target's center mass, head, or pelvis. You must clearly see and focus on the front sight.

When you are close to a target, within a few feet, you can visually align the barrel while maintaining your precision. The more you train the further away you will be able to achieve good alignment without the use of sights. More times than not, precision is more important than speed. If you practice for precision, speed will come. If you practice for speed, however, precision may never follow. "Smooth is fast."

Aligning the Sights

As mentioned above, your eye(s) and the sights and the target all have to be lined up.

> **Training Tip:** You can only shoot as fast as you can see.

The front sight must be centered in the notch of the rear sight, left to right. The top of the front sight should align with the top of the notch, as well as with the target.

There is a straight line between your eye and your target. Your job is to move the sights onto that line as quickly and precisely as possible. If you start moving your head, you are changing the line; and it is much more difficult to line up four objects than two.

Once your sights are aligned, focus on the front sight only, letting the rear sight and the target go out of focus while you press the trigger back. You will still be able to see the rear sight and the target clearly enough to know if either moves significantly, but it is the front sight that tells you whether the muzzle is on target.

Remember, this all happens very quickly. Unless your threat is stationary and unsuspecting, you don't have time to fine-tune your sight alignment until it is perfect.

How and Where to Aim

An accurate shot requires the weapon be held so that the trajectory coincides sufficiently with the intended point of impact at the moment the round leaves the barrel. Ensuring that sufficient weapon alignment is maintained until the round leaves the barrel is largely a matter of trigger control.

Typically, aiming is taught by superimposing correct sight alignment on the target and achieving a proper sight picture. Since improper sight alignment creates angular errors, the proper relationship between front and rear sights requires a great deal of practice.

Precision sighted aiming—front sight centered in the rear sight notch, tip of the front sight level with the top of the rear sight, the shooter focusing on the front site—can certainly facilitate hitting the intended target with precision. However, it is limiting, often more precise than what is required and quite often much too slow for defensive shooting.

Defensive shooting with a handgun can at times require extreme precision; for example, the threat who is a good distance away, or one who exposes only a small part of his body from behind cover, or a low-light situation. In these situations, precision fire may be required. However, most real world encounters demand less precision and commensurately more speed.

Newer shooters are often pleasantly surprised at the level of accuracy that can be achieved without the perfect sight picture. For instance, it is possible to make a head shot at two meters across a large room, with misaligned sights. I recommend that you prove this to yourself by doing the following drill.

From two meters, fire one round with the front sight perfectly located in the rear notch, one with the edge of the front sight touching one side of the notch, one with the other edge of the front sight against the other side of the notch, one with the tip of the front sight barely showing above the bottom of the notch, and one with the front sight high. Hold the tip of the front sight on the same spot for every shot. Provided you have proper trigger control, your group should be no more than four inches in diameter, which is well within the scope of combat accuracy.

It is possible to see the sights and note their alignment with your focus on the target, rather than the front sight, or somewhere between the front sight and target. Both sights will be somewhat blurry, but if they offer sufficient contrast, they will still provide the information you need to make an effective hit. Given that your natural tendency under duress will be to look at the threat anyway, this type of aiming is a very useful defensive skill, and shifting your focus toward the threat will greatly enhance your situational awareness.

At close range you can even use the outline of the rear of the weapon as your "sight." If you see the top or side of the gun, you know it is tilted up or to one side, respectively. Conversely, if everything looks symmetrical, the bore is probably aligned well enough with the target to make a good hit at room ranges.

The thinner the pistol, the better the directional information it provides. Hence single-stack semis offer better feedback in this regard than those with double-column magazines.

Front sight focus is often unnecessary in close-range handgun combat scenarios and attempting to obtain a perfect sight picture for every shot under such conditions will often slow you down to an unacceptable level. Learn what constitutes an acceptable sight picture for different situations. For every person it will be different. All shooters should learn at what distance they can point-shoot, use the outline of the weapon, and when they need to take the time for a well-aimed shot.

See what *you* need to see to make the hit. Novice shooters are usually taught to just concentrate on the front sight, since this is the first step in the process of developing the ability to "feel" when the weapon is aligned.

The front sight is a valuable reference, being located just above the muzzle. Allowing your focus to drift downrange while remaining aware of sight picture is more of an advanced technique that all shooters should work toward.

You do need some source of weapon alignment information. The sights provide a significant percentage of feedback when practicing the different visual techniques. A proper sight picture can serve as "training wheels," a visual template that can train your body to align the weapon with the target when you can't or don't see the sights clearly.

Even when you do not see the sights, you still must positively identify your target. It might be possible to shoot at a sound or a muzzle flash, as is often done in military combat, but the legal and moral aspect of threat identification as stated in Safety Rule #4 would be violated.

To become faster at visually verified aiming, you will have to be quick at seeing the relationship of your weapon and the target. You can become quite adept at confirming an acceptable sight picture with time. As you gain experience, you will actually learn to see things faster.

As an alternative to a center mass shot, when confronting a potential threat (armed with anything other than a gun) and assuming you have enough distance to do so without undue risk of being disarmed, consider aiming at the threat's pelvis. From this position, you can see the threat's hands. And if need be you can either fire immediately or track up his centerline to center mass.

Point-Shooting

Point-shooting is finally making its resurgence. It is fast and works extremely well when the tactical situation is relatively simple, straightforward, and takes place within close proximity.

It is irrational thinking to suggest that we will be able to force ourselves to focus on our front sight, never mind align the front and rear sights, when someone up close and personal is trying to kill us.

Every instinct and survival mechanism tells us to focus on the threat—to look at the person who is up close and trying to kill us so we can respond to his actions. When our lives are threatened, we look at the thing or person causing the threat. Humans have millions of years of evolution telling us to do just that in a fight. Trying to look at your sights in such situations is likely to be counter to millions of years of evolution.

Point-shooting is reasonably accurate at close ranges. Remember, approximately 75 percent of gunfights happen within three meters.

> **Training Tip:** In most pistol confrontations you will most likely not have time to find your sights and your target, which will most likely be 21 feet or less away.

Sighted shooting is a complex and fine motor skill. Point-shooting is a gross motor skill, and, as we discussed, we try to reduce fine motor skills from our tactical toolbox.

A great deal of point-shooting documentation and training comes from the work of Colonel Rex Applegate and Michael Janich. It was developed and refined during periods of actual violent combat and not on a training range or in a classroom.

At the turn of the century Police Captains William Fairbairn and Eric Sykes were sent to Shanghai, China, which at the time was a very tough town. Together, they created a complete close-quarters combat program that included firearms skills and tactics needed to combat the threats that they would go up against on a daily basis. The firearms techniques they taught their fellow officers were based on real world needs, simplicity, and ease of training. They were only interested in what worked, and what would save lives. The most notable aspect of their techniques was the fact that they relied on natural physiological responses of human beings under stress. One-handed, non-sighted fire was their primary method for dealing with the up-close threats.

Fairbairns and Sykes' method of point-shooting, using one hand, was quickly proven to be the quickest, most natural, and easiest-to-teach method of defensive shooting at close contact distances—which was the most common type of combat scenario in Shanghai during this time.

In the early 1940s, Colonel Rex Applegate, familiar with Fairbairn and Sykes' techniques and their effectiveness, instituted them as the primary training system for the U.S. troops during World War II.

For their firearms training, Applegate taught military personnel how to use one-handed point-shooting to hit targets at up to 50 meters very quickly with very little training. This technique was simply pointing the weapon one handed at the target while focusing on the target over the gun's slide. The weapon was brought up to line of sight, under control and using a straight arm, with the strong foot forward.

"Proper training in point-shooting achieves quicker expertise, does not necessitate so much retraining to maintain proficiency, saves more law enforcement lives, and takes criminals permanently off the streets."

—Colonel Rex Applegate

Many of the servicemen who went through Applegate's program ended up using these point-shooting techniques and survived many deadly encounters during the course of the war.

Fairbairn conducted extensive research on the subject and was actually involved in over two hundred gunfights himself, perpetuating his reputation as being the inspiration of James Bond.

During his career he developed tactics and training procedures that are still used and practiced today. In 1942, he was sent to the United States to work with Colonel William "Wild Bill" Donovan to assist with the development of the Office of Strategic Services, the predecessor of the Central Intelligence Agency.

Point-shooting dates back before Fairbain and Sykes, a fact that was affirmed when Applegate found an old letter written to Wild Bill Hickok. The letter was from someone asking Hickock how he killed all of those men. Hickock's response was that he raised his hand to his eye level, like pointing a finger, and he fired. This letter was just one of the many affirmations these point-shooting innovators were receiving. Fairbairn, in particular, also did extensive research on law enforcement shootings and combat shootings and spent years on this research learning what worked and what didn't work in gunfights. He studied the shooting reports from allied troops, enemy troops, and our government personnel.

The majority of weapons instructors still train to shoot using only sighted techniques despite the fact that it has been extensively documented that a vast majority of all shootings take place within "three meters, three rounds, and three seconds". All of our data and

Training Tip: In defensive shooting, studies indicate that law enforcement do not look at their sights. Almost all studies show that police officers not only did not see their sights, but many of them did not even see the weapon in their own hands. All they did was shoot until the threat was neutralized. Without sufficient training, you will most likely miss the vast majority of your targets. Instinctive shooting, without seeing the sights, is probably how you will shoot in defense.

research indicate that there is little to no time for the sighted techniques in most gunfights. We also know that most of the best shooters in the world, who are well trained in sighted techniques, revert back to unsighted point-shooting in a gunfight.

Point-shooting is easy to comprehend, easy to learn, and it doesn't take as much time or ammunition to become proficient. Point-shooting was created for the one-handed shooter, but many shooters now use two hands. Point-shooting also works really well with small, concealable guns, some of which have small sights or no sights at all.

Point-shooting Steps:
- Crouch deeply, which also makes you a smaller target.
- Lunge toward the threat facing it squarely.
- Focus the eyes on the threat and not the sights and do not shift your focus from target to front sight as you would in a well-aimed, front-sight-focus, proper-sight-alignment shot.
- Extend the non-dominant hand to the side for balance.
- Acquire a good firm "convulsive" one- or two-handed grip.
- Grasp the weapon in alignment with the forearm, at the end of a fully extended arm.
- Keep a rigid wrist and elbow.
- Raise the weapon into the line of sight as though the arm were a pump handle.

- Fire the weapon by squeezing the entire hand as it enters the line of sight.
- Shoot at center mass, pelvis, or head.

Point-shooting relies on the body's instinctive ability to point at objects with "reasonable accuracy." The ability to point at targets has been practiced by us all since our early childhood. It is a gross motor skill that does not deteriorate. The muzzle of the weapon simply replaces the pointing finger. It is important to note point-shooting is not sighted fire, it is "aimed" fire.

With point-shooting, you do not need to concern yourself with a smooth press on the trigger. The "convulsive" type grip often used in point shooting tolerates a faster/jerkier trigger squeeze.

The alignment of the barrel when point-shooting should align with the bones of the forearm. When the weapon is held with the two-handed grip, the alignment of the barrel with the bones of the forearm can cause the weapon to point off-center toward the non-dominant-hand side. This is an issue of concern for point-shooters who bring the weapon to the midline of the body.

You will experience emotional and physical responses when dealing with a threat wanting to take your life. These responses are instinctive gross motor movements that will most likely override your ability to perform any fine motor skills.

There are as many reasons to train using sighted techniques as there are reasons to train in point-shooting. The research behind point-shooting is well documented and extensive. Regardless, you will still hear some instructors who discard this type of training.

One thing I learned from doing my research is that many shooting instructors only teach what they understand and what works best for them, which often excludes point-shooting. There are a lot of great weapons and tactics instructors out there. Many of them have been in combat, others were or are law enforcement officers and have been in shootouts and others are IPSC or IDPA champions. My point is that they all have something to offer but not one of them should be the sole one-stop source when it comes to doing your research.

Since point-shooting is the method and natural tendency most often used in a gunfight, it should be practiced in training. Very few weapons courses spend much time if any on this much-needed skill.

Flash Front Sight Picture

When acquiring a flash front sight picture, you are basically just looking over the rear sight while briefly looking at the front sight.

Even Jeff Cooper, the "dean of sighted shooting," used to teach that most shooters solely rely on their highly refined pointing ability to put the weapon on target and use a "flash front sight picture" rather than aligning the sights on the target. The sights, he said, should only be used to confirm that the weapon is already on target.

> **Training Tip:** It is difficult to get a good sight picture when your head, eyes, and hands are all moving at the same time. Eliminate your head and eyes from moving.

Most shooters agree that at "longer" distances—usually past 2–5 meters depending on the shooter, sighted shooting must be used in order to ensure combat accuracy.

Logic and experience indicate that if we train in sighted shooting to an acceptable level we'll develop the kinesthetic alignment, the "muscle memory," to point-shoot with reasonable accuracy.

In any gunfight, there will be an inherent trade-off between speed and accuracy. At longer distances you are gambling with point-shooting so you'll want to use your front sight or at least flash front sight.

Cirillo's Silhouette Point Shooting

Jim Cirillo, the legendary member of the New York City Police Department "Stake Out Squad," taught that when using sights, the conscious mind is focused on the sight picture, while the subconscious mind takes in the nuances of how the gun looks when it is aligned on the target.

Cirillo taught this method by taping over the sights of the weapon, and demonstrating what the gun looks like in alignment and out of alignment. He taught aiming solely by using the shape of the weapon and found that many shooters actually shot better with the sights taped. Since the shooter does not see a sight picture, they typically don't jerk the trigger when they think they have the perfect sight picture. By relying on the subconscious mind rather than the conscious mind, shooters are able to get the weapon aligned and shots fired quicker, especially in lower light.

To use this method, simply place the silhouette of the gun over the area of the target. The silhouette point-shooting method is effective up to 10 meters and works better with semis than with revolvers.

MULTIPLE SHOTS

"Defensive situations are almost always emergencies, so we must put considerable emphasis on speed. The weapon must be fired quickly (but accurately), and the shooter must always automatically prepare to fire again quickly."
—John S. Farnham

You always need to be ready to take another shot. In defensive shooting, we train to shoot until the threat is neutralized and this often requires multiple shots, especially when using a pistol. A one-shot stop with a pistol is very rare. If you happen to get lucky and place a round in the "fatal T" (the area between eyes and down to sternum) then maybe you will get the rare one-shot stop. But do not count on it. To ensure accurate multiple effective hits on your target you must be able to manipulate the trigger with minimal disturbances of the front sight.

Shooting is most effective when it's "rhythmic." The trigger should be reset at the same speed it was retracted, the sights should be realigned on the target's desired point of impact, and you must prepare for a next shot—even if you don't end up needing it.

The Controlled Pair

Most likely when using a handgun one shot is not enough to neutralize a threat. The chances of achieving your desired results are much greater with a "controlled pair." After the first shot is fired, refocus on the front sight, prep the trigger, and allow for a surprise break for the following shot. Each shot is a controlled, individual shot and requires a separate sight picture and a separate surprise break even when executed quickly. Since we are always prepping for additional shots, two shots require three sight pictures, three shots require four sight pictures, etc.

Rapid-Fire Shooting

Since our objective as defensive shooters includes neutralizing the threat, rapid multiple shots are often required when using a handgun. Your training should include these rapid-fire techniques:

Rapid-fire shooting—notice the severe muzzle flip.

Trigger Control

- Regardless of the speed at which you're shooting, the trigger must be pressed straight to the rear and not pushed or pulled to the side during the trigger manipulation. Keep an equal amount of pressure across the face on the trigger. Keep the pressure in the middle of the trigger as you press straight back.
- Keep the pad of the finger more or less to the face of the trigger as you press.
- Only allow the distal joint (near tip of finger) of the finger to move during the trigger press.

Bob Munden, known as "the fastest shooter of all time," shooting his famed revolver.

Slide lock—time for a speed reload

Speed

- The speed at which you press the trigger will depend on your training, your weapon, the light conditions, your distance from the target and the size of the target.
- Regardless of the circumstances, press and release the trigger at the same speed, using rhythm.

Brian Enos

Brian Enos

Effort

- Use just enough force to overcome the resistance of the trigger. Imagine gently touching the rear of the trigger against the frame as you press back.

FOLLOW-THROUGH AND SCAN

Follow-through

Follow-through is a very important and often neglected fundamental. Before this point was emphasized in shooting courses, shooters would often shoot at their targets, scan and quickly holster without ensuring the desired results were met, e.g., the threat was neutralized. They skipped the vital step of follow-through after the shot was fired. The old "double tap" drills were notorious for skipping follow-through. The shooter simply shot two quick rounds and moved on to another target or holstered.

> **Training Tip:**
> More shots are lost after the firing pin hits the round than before (poor follow-through).

Follow-through is controlling the weapon and the trigger after the trigger breaks and ensuring your shots achieved the desired results. This also helps the shooter avoid disturbing the alignment of the pistol.

When the trigger breaks, maintain your focus on the front sight, and keep finger contact on the trigger as you hold it to the rear. Before moving your weapon off target, ensure you have achieved your desired results. Just because you shot at the threat does not mean he has been neutralized. You may have missed; you may have hit him but did not stop him; he may be wearing body armor; or he may be on drugs and the rounds made no effect.

When firing a shot, you will visually lose the front sight momentarily on recoil and will need to immediately regain front sight focus

Author scanning before holstering

as soon as the recoil dissipates. Do not release the trigger until the recoil cycle is complete. Maintain finger contact on the trigger and hold it to the rear as the shot is fired. Release it only after you have reacquired the front sight. Even then, only release the trigger far enough to "reset" it. You will hear the trigger reset when dry firing, and will feel the "click" as you begin to release. This is as far as you need to go in order to fire multiple shots. By allowing the trigger to move any further forward you will increase the recovery time between shots.

> **Note:** It's important to recognize that more shots are lost after the firing pin hits the round than before.

The ability to fire multiple controlled shots is extremely important in a tactical situation. Except for special circumstances, such as a single, one-stop shot in the "fatal T," expect to fire multiple times.

Scan

"Scan" is not considered a "weapons fundamental" but is always conducted after the follow-through. This is an important step since so many attacks involve more than just one threat. After you have dealt with your threat, scan and look for others who may have emerged. Many shooters experience tunnel vision in life-threatening situations. As you are neutralizing one threat, his buddies may emerge and unless you actively look for additional threats, you risk dropping your guard or even holstering too soon. You do not want to holster until you know your threat has been neutralized and there are not any other threats in your vicinity.

Scanning is accomplished by dropping the weapon slightly so you can see over the sights. As you scan, your weapon can follow your eyes, or your weapon can remain at the ready.

When scanning, be sure to look behind you.

LOADING, RELOADING, AND UNLOADING

When initially loading any weapon always do so with safety in mind. It is best to load on a range while facing downrange and keeping the weapon in a safe direction. But that is not always possible. You may load your weapon in a vehicle, in your home, or elsewhere. Always load keeping all safety rules in mind.

Author reaching for a new magazine.
Note the straight finger which he uses to index the magazine.

Reloading on the move. When possible, reload behind cover.

A novice shooter will often bury his head and will look down at the weapon when loading, reloading, or correcting malfunctions. This can easily become a very bad habit. You become an easier target when you're focusing your attention on reloading or fixing a malfunction rather than on your threat. It's a lot easier for someone to shoot at you if you are not shooting back.

As I often tell my students, "A person moving is difficult to hit, a person moving to cover is more difficult to hit, and a person moving to cover while shooting back is the most difficult to hit. You should be the latter."

Eyes off target and burying head down into the weapon

Why would you slowly reload your weapon or correct a malfunction with an administrative, lackadaisical mind-set, rather than with purpose and a combat mind-set during training, when in a real life encounter you would be doing it as fast as possible? Conduct every reload and correct every malfunction as a practice for the gunfight you must win.

Brian Enos reloading faster than the eye can see

Four things can prevent your weapon from firing: a broken weapon, forgetting to disengage the safety, malfunctions, and lack of rounds.

You must always ensure your weapon is in good working condition and understand how it operates. You also need to know what to do when it doesn't fire; how to correct malfunctions under highly stressful circumstances; and how to load and reload quickly and effectively.

Weapon reloads are classified as administrative reloads, speed reloads, and tactical reloads. Loading, reloading, and unloading require a great deal of practice. The procedures below are the

*Author
conducting
a speed
reload from
the ready
position*

methods I recommend and teach to U.S. and foreign governments and military communities.

You may need to slightly modify these steps, depending on the size of your hand, coordination, etc. You will want to develop your own techniques by practicing the steps until you are comfortable doing them and do not have to look down at the weapon. If any of these actions still feel awkward after repetitive practice, then you need to adapt, adjust, or replace that specific action with a technique that works better for you.

Semiautomatic Reloading

Semiautomatic Administrative Reloading

The administrative reload is used in non-combat situations. The weapon does not leave the holster during the process.

- The administrative reload is typically done with the weapon in the slide-forward configuration.

Author conducting a reload with a "wounded hand."

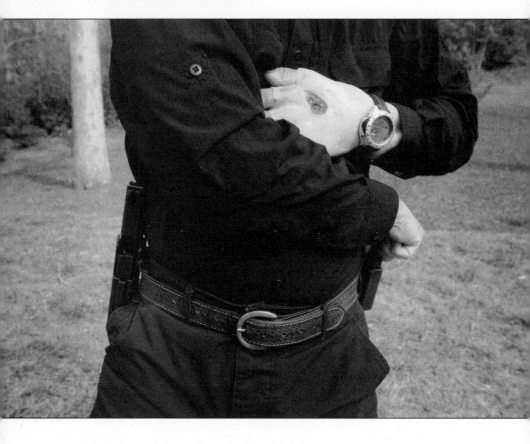

- With the weapon still in the holster, simply reach back and release the magazine.
- Place the ejected magazine in a rear pouch or, if necessary, in a pocket (since the magazine is not full). The problem I have with putting partially used magazines in a pocket is that if in a prone, kneeling, or awkward shooting position, it can be very difficult to retrieve these magazines in a hurry.
- With your support hand, reach for the new magazine from your magazine pouch the same way every time. When you take one from its pouch, seat its base in your palm and hold it with your index finger along its front side. Holding the magazine this way gives you maximum control when inserting it into the magazine well.

- Always remove your magazines in the same logical order, designating the pouches sequentially. For instance, pouch 1 is closest to the belt buckle, pouch 2 is next to it, and so on. Always train by drawing the magazine from pouch 1 first. If magazine pouch 1 is empty then go to pouch 2. This keeps you from wasting valuable time searching for magazines; and you'll always know exactly where they are and how many magazines you have left. This also ensures you will always reach for the same place. If the magazine is not there because of an earlier reload, you will know to move to the next sequential pouch quickly and with certainty.
- Bring the fresh magazine to the holstered weapon so the flat back of it touches the flat back of the magazine well, and roll the front up to align fully with the entrance to the well. You will already be very close to the proper angle when it touches, and the roll will be minimal. The point here is that you align the back of the magazine with the well first, not the front.
- Once the magazine is aligned with the well, which you will know when you can start moving it up into the well smoothly, seat it with a swift and sure motion.
- You should feel and hear the click when the magazine is fully seated.
- Push and pull on the magazine to ensure it is seated.
- A round should still be chambered.

Semiautomatic Speed Reloading

The speed reload is the most practical, the quickest, and most used reload during a gunfight. With adequate training, it can be done in less than two seconds, without having to take your eyes off the threat(s).

The following are steps for speed reloading Semiautomatic weapons from the ready position. Some shooters angle their muzzles slightly upward if that can be considered a safe direction based on the surroundings when loading, reloading, or correcting malfunctions. The weapon would normally be in the slide-locked-to-the-

Author conducting a speed reload

Shooting instructor Jim C. conducting a speed reload from the kneeling position.

Instructor Jim C. conducting a speed reload while kneeling.

Time for a speed reload

rear configuration; the reason a speed reload is conducted is because the weapon went dry, which typically locks the slide to the rear in most Semiautomatic weapons.

• It is very important to always keep a visual on the threat. Train so you do not have to look down at the weapon. This will also be very helpful in low-light situations, since you may not be able to see your weapon anyway. If necessary you can quickly glance at the weapon, while still keeping peripheral vision on the threat and the environment.

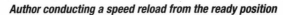

Author conducting a speed reload from the ready position

- Maintain your good shooting grip to be ready to shoot. Even during a reload, yours should be dry for less than two seconds.
- Maintain a straight finger throughout the loading process.

- With your support hand, reach for the new magazine from your magazine pouch the same way every time. When you take one from its pouch, seat its base in your palm and hold it with your index finger along its front side. Holding the magazine this way gives you maximum control when inserting it into the magazine well.

- Always remove your magazines in the same logical order, designating the pouches sequentially. For instance, pouch 1 is closest to the belt buckle, pouch 2 is next to it and so on. Always train by drawing the magazine from pouch 1 first. If magazine pouch

1 is empty then go to pouch 2. This keeps you from wasting valuable time searching for magazines; and you'll always know exactly where they are and how many magazines you have left. This also ensures you will always reach for the same place. If the magazine is not there because of an earlier reload, you will know to move to the next sequential pouch quickly and with certainty.

Again, every second counts in a gunfight and everything we do in training is to prepare to win a gunfight.

- Move the magazine to the weapon, not the weapon to the magazine.

- Bring the fresh magazine up so the flat back of it touches the flat back of the magazine well, and roll the front up to align fully with the entrance to the well. You will already be very close to the proper angle when it touches, and the roll will be minimal. The point here is that you align the back of the magazine with the well first, not the front.

- Once the magazine is aligned with the well, which you will know when you can start moving it up into the well smoothly, seat it with a swift and sure motion. Use the palm of your support hand (the one holding the magazine) to seat it with most of the pres-

sure on the front of the magazine base. If you push against the rear of the base, your hand can run into your shooting hand or

the frame of the weapon, which can disrupt the smooth seating
of the magazine.
*   With a good grip on the slide, pull the slide all the way to the rear
    until it hits the frame assertively, cycling the slide.

- How you hold the slide depends on whether you are left-handed or right-handed. In either case, your shooting hand maintains control of the weapon, and your support hand manipulates the slide.
- As soon as the slide hits the frame, release it. The weapon should be horizontal at this point. Do not "ride the slide" forward; let the spring action do its work. Riding the slide will slow down

the action and can cause a malfunction. Letting the slide go also frees up your other hand so you can go into a two-handed grip immediately.

If you have an external safety, use caution as some safeties, especially those that are ambidextrous, as it can be set to the "on" position by mistake when you initially grip the slide.

Author reloading from the prone position

- As soon as the weapon is reloaded bring it to the "up" position and conduct a good scan. You may have been a bit distracted during the reload and may have missed something of potential significance, e.g., the threat has moved to another location, or another threat appeared.

Instructor Jim C. conducting a tactical reload

Semiautomatic Tactical Reloading

A tactical reload is conducted during a lull or break in the action, especially if you expect more exchange of fire. When possible you will want to reload before the last round is actually fired and you end up holding an empty weapon.

For example: You are in a gunfight, and you have exchanged fire with a threat. You have good cover but feel it is to your tactical advantage to either advance to or retreat from the threat. In either case, you are moving from one position of cover to another, and do not want to get caught without ammo running between cover. You have shot a number of rounds, but since we no longer count the rounds we fire (this went out in the '80s), you have no idea how many rounds are left in the magazine. So you simply keep a round chambered, bring up a fresh magazine and quickly exchange it with

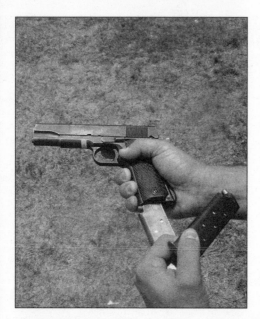

The fine motor skill of conducting a tactical reload

the partial magazine. You never go empty. Now you feel it is safe to move from cover, across a danger area, to new cover.

Alternatively, you can also perform a modified speed reload, and pick up the ejected partial magazine after it drops. You will probably want to do this in the kneeling position if the situation permits, as it will be faster, the magazine will be easier to find and pick up, and you will be a smaller target. Keep in mind, searching for a magazine during a gunfight is not the best use of your time, especially if it is dark, you are moving, you're in deep grass, or are on or near the water.

Author conducting a tactical reload from the ready position

A tactical reload is a fine motor skill and does take quite a bit of practice to perfect.

Semiautomatic Tactical Reload Steps:

- From the ready position or with the muzzle angled slightly upward (if that can be considered a safe direction).
- The weapon would normally be in the slide-forward configuration since it has not run dry.
- Keep your eyes on the threat. Train so you do not have to look down at the weapon. It is very important to always try to keep a visual on the threat. This will also be very helpful in low-light

situations, since you may not be able to see your weapon in the low light anyway. If necessary you can quickly glance at the weapon, while still keeping peripheral vision on the threat and the environment.

- Do not let go of your good shooting grip. Be ready to shoot, especially during a tactical reload. This is one of its great advantages since the weapon is always ready to fire and has not gone dry.
- With your support hand, reach for the new magazine from your magazine pouch the same way every time. When you take one from its pouch, seat its base in your palm and hold it with your index

finger along its front side. Holding the magazine this way gives you maximum control when inserting it into the magazine well.

- Always remove your magazines in the same logical order, designating the pouches sequentially. For instance, pouch 1 is closest to the belt buckle, pouch 2 is next to it, and so on. Always train by drawing the magazine from pouch 1 first. If magazine pouch 1 is empty then go to pouch 2. This keeps you from wasting valuable time searching for magazines; and you'll always know exactly where they are and how many magazines you have left. This also ensures you will always reach for the same place. If the

magazine is not there because of an earlier reload, you will know to move to the next sequential pouch quickly and with certainty. Again, every second counts in a gunfight and everything we do in training is to prepare to win a gunfight.

- Move the magazine to the weapon, not the weapon to the magazine.

- Always handle the magazines the same way. When you take one from its pouch with your support hand, seat its base in your palm and hold it with your index finger along its front side.

Holding the magazine this way gives you maximum control when inserting it into the magazine well.

- Bring the new magazine up to the magazine well and only then press the magazine release. (If you do not have a spare magazine, don't release the used one.) Hold the magazine vertically, parallel

with the grip and slightly below it. Holding the weapon upright allows the used magazine to drop out from the magazine well.

- Instead of letting the magazine drop, pull it and stop it from falling with the palm of the hand holding the new magazine.

- Use two fingers of that hand to pull the magazine from the well and hold it while inserting and seating the fresh magazine. Then store the partially used magazine in an empty magazine pouch or pocket if necessary.
- Once the magazine is aligned with the well, which you will know when you can start moving it up into the well smoothly, seat it with a swift and sure motion. Use the palm of your support hand (the one holding the magazine) to seat it with most of the pressure on the front of the magazine base. If you push against the rear of the base, your hand can run into your shooting hand or the frame of the weapon, which can disrupt the smooth seating of the magazine.

- You should not have to look at your weapon, your hands, or your magazine while reloading. This is something you should learn through practice. Your eyes have more important things to do, e.g., keeping an eye on the threat and the situation as it unfolds.
- Press checks are not conducted during a tactical reload!

Semiautomatic Unloading

There are four main actions required when unloading a semi-auto pistol:

- Eject the magazine—always remove the source first.
- Keep the weapons pointed in a safe direction, cycle the slide (two to three times) to eject the chambered round.
- Lock the slide to the rear.
- Check the chamber twice, both visually and physically, ensuring you have a safe and empty weapon.

Semiautomatic Press-checks

Press-checks are never done after a speed or tactical reload. They are only done when you have the time and want a bit of insurance by knowing a round has been chambered e.g., after initially loading the weapon.

- When conducting a press-check, use your non-shooting hand to partially retract the slide to look for brass. In low- and no-light situations you may not see the brass and will have to feel it with the tip of your finger. Some Semiautomatic pistols, such as the newer Glocks, have chamber indicators, which are a quick way to tell if a round has been chambered or not.
- During the press-check, you need to modify your grip on the slide.
- Be sure to keep the weapon at the ready position and keep a straight finger when conducting a press check.

Back side of magazine has to be inserted first

Revolver Reloading

Steps

- Hold the revolver horizontally where the cylinder swings upward and toward you for best control.
- Press the cylinder latch, then hold the weapon in your non-shooting hand while you open the cylinder. Your shooting (dominant) hand is more dexterous and faster for reloading.
- Keep the cylinder from rotating. There is a cylinder cutout in the frame to put a finger through, which allows you to do this.
- Point the muzzle upward, and hit the ejector rod with the palm of your shooting hand. Hit it, instead of just pushing it, to be sure of ejecting all the shell cases. You can kill someone unintentionally with an un-ejected shell.
- Point the muzzle down, and load new rounds or use a speed loader to load a full cylinder's worth of cartridges at once. If you are using a speed-loader, let it do the work. Just line up two rounds, and the rest will follow. Let the speed loader drop into place, and hit the release.
- Be sure when you withdraw the speed loader, you do not draw the rounds out of the cylinder with it. Discard the speed loader. Maybe later, after the fight, you can retrieve it, but for the moment, let it go.
- After reloading a revolver, shift it back to your shooting hand and spin the cylinder. If it does not spin freely, open it up and make sure no shells are protruding above the cylinder wall. Look for any dirt or sludge that might have crept in. Then close it and try it again.

Author conducting a reload with a "wounded hand"

Lock the slide to the rear using your holster, belt buckle, or shoe.

Revolver Tactical Reloading

Steps

- It is also possible to do a tactical reload with a revolver, by simply replacing the spent shells with new ones. Shell casings expand when fired, so if you point the muzzle downward, and ease the ejector rod up instead of smacking it, the spent cases will protrude from the cylinder while the unspent shells will slip back down when the ejector rod is released.

The "tap" portion of a tap-rack can be done on your knee or foot.

- Pick out the spent shells and replace them with new ones. This procedure takes longer, so be sure you have time to complete it before starting. If time is an issue, go for a speed load.
- Your life may depend on your having versatility and agility with this maneuver; you may need to accomplish it with one hand as well as with speed and efficiency, without needing to see what you're doing with your hands.

One-Handed Reloading
(Semiautomatic or Revolver)

- You will want to practice one-handed reloading in case you are wounded or otherwise have one hand occupied.
- There are different ways to work the slide on semis using your belt or shoe or other objects.
- Practice manipulating the ejector rod and cylinder on a revolver with one hand, and propping up the gun against your body for loading.

When practicing weapon skills, concentrate on conducting every skill set correctly and with certainty. If you are smooth, you will be fast. Speed will come naturally with repetition. Like with any weapon skill, efficiency begins with deliberate movements which are perfected through repetition and practicing perfect practice.

MALFUNCTIONS

We often say in the shooting community that hearing a *click* when you should hear a *bang* can be as deadly as hearing a *bang* when you should hear a *click*. Jams, the term our friends in the SAS and the SBS like to use, are mechanical failures requiring disassembly of the weapon. Malfunctions, which are much more common than jams, are generally "stoppages" that can be cleared by the shooter.

It may be important to note that the reason some people prefer revolvers over semis is that malfunctions are typically not an issue with revolvers. When a round does not fire, the procedure is simply to pull the trigger again; the cylinder spins and a new round moves into place.

In this chapter we will look at the malfunctions or stoppages most often encountered when firing semi-autos. A clear mind and some relatively simple manipulations will clear most semi-auto malfunctions. Most law enforcement and military personnel carry both a primary weapon and a secondary weapon as a backup. Having a backup weapon is generally the fastest response to a weapon that malfunctions or runs dry. Malfunctions are generally categorized into phases or types. Some weapon trainers classify them into two and some into three. I prefer discussing three types when teaching.

Author clearing a type-one malfunction—"Failure to Fire"

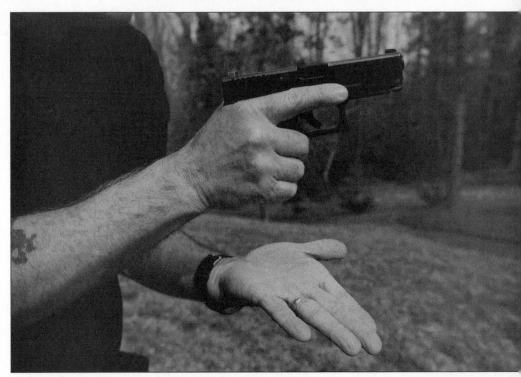

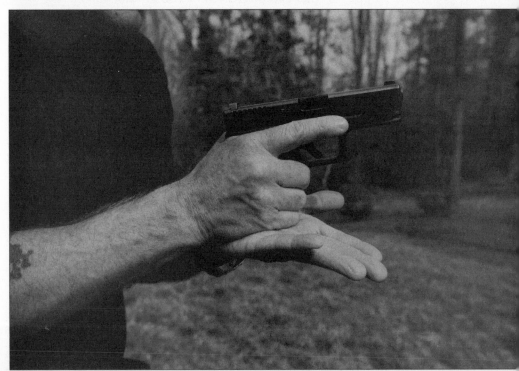

Type-One Malfunctions—"Failure to Fire"

Type-one malfunctions are also called "failure to fire" malfunctions and are characterized by the phrase "when all you hear is a deafening click."

Possible causes include:

- Round in chamber fails to fire
- Magazine not fully seated when slide went forward
- Magazine release was inadvertently hit
- Empty magazine
- Fatigued spring in magazine
- Broken follower in magazine
- Reciprocation of slide does not strip a live cartridge from the magazine
- No round in the chamber
- Bad ammo
- Bad or moist primer
- Light strike

Procedures for clearing Type-One Malfunctions

"Tap, Rack, Assess"

- Tap magazine on base plate to seat it into the magazine well.
- Grasp slide with fingers away from and not covering muzzle or ejection port.
- Pull slide rearward and release slide (rack). Do not ride the slide forward.
- Reacquire a good two-handed grip without sweeping the support hand with the muzzle.
- Be certain not to reverse the order. You must tap first and then rack.
- Assess the situation, from the ready position.

Note: Shooters used to use the phrase "tap, rack, bang," but changed it to "tap, rack, assess." Too many shooters were trained to "bang" as soon as they racked. This was a problem because too many times a "bang" was not required, but in every case an "assess" was required. You do need to quickly get back to the ready position and scan/assess to see if you may have missed anything of significance while you were clearing your malfunction.

Type-Two Malfunctions—"Stove Pipe"

Type-two malfunctions are also called "stove pipe" malfunctions and are characterized by: the shell casing not fully ejecting causing the casing to stick up in full view; failure of the case to extract and eject; the round not fully ejecting out of the ejection port.

Possible causes include:

- Bad ejector
- Bad extractor
- Bad ejector and bad extractor combined
- Wrist injury

Type-two malfunction—"stove pipe"

- Improper grip
- Limp wristing

Procedures for Correcting Type-Two Malfunctions

- Tap the magazine base to ensure it is seated.
- Rack the slide and release so the new round will chamber. This should rid the spent casing from the slide.
- Do not ride the slide forward.

Author clearing stove pipe using the sweeping method.

Type-Three Malfunctions—"Double Feed"

Type-three malfunctions are also known as "double feeds" and are characterized by: a failure to extract, eject and load; the pistol firing but the case does not clear the chamber as the slide reciprocates;

Author clearing a "type-three malfunction—double feed"

after a complete rearward motion, the slide starting to move forward and striping the next round from the magazine, which starts forward and strikes the already-fired cartridge case that's still in the chamber area; two rounds appearing to be chambered at the same time.

Possible causes include:
- Faulty, dirty, or bad extractors
- Faulty, dirty, or bad ejectors

- Faulty, dirty or bad magazines.
- Bad ammunition
- Dirty weapon
- Improper grip

Procedure for Correcting Type-Three Malfunctions

- This malfunction is more complicated than the rest, but "stay in the fight" and fix the weapon. There may be no other choice if that is your only weapon.

Tapping magazine in place by tapping weapon on knee

Locking slide with Kydex holster

Locking slide with Kydex holster

- Tap magazine to ensure it is fully seated
- Attempt to rack the slide
- If you are unable to "tap, rack" then proceed to the following additional steps.
- Lock the slide to the rear. It may be locked up and appear to be locked to the rear, but most often, it is not actually locked.

- Tilt the weapon so ejection side port is down allowing gravity to assist you while working the slide with the support hand.
- Strip out the magazine and place it under your shooting arm.
- Grasp slide.

- Rack the slide two to three times to clear the obstruction. Hopefully you will see and/or hear the round eject from the weapon.
- Replace the magazine with a fresh magazine.

- If you reach for a fresh magazine and find you do not have one, simply use the one you tucked under your shooting arm. The rounds in the magazine will most likely have to be straightened out with your support hand before it can be put back into the magazine well.

Author conducting a speed reload

- If you do have a fresh magazine, use it, and the magazine placed under your arm will just drop to the ground as you bring your weapon to the "ready" or "up" position.
- Tap, rack, and assess.

Author clearing a type-three malfunction—"double feed"—with a wounded hand.

General Malfunction and Reloading Notes

- Be sure to the check barrel, slide, and receiver serial numbers to ensure that they match before firing any weapon.
- Do not correct the malfunction (or reload) at full arm extension—a mistake made by many novice shooters. Correct all malfunctions and all reloads at the ready position.
- Do not block your vision with your weapon while fixing a malfunction or reloading.
- Do not look at your weapon while correcting malfunctions or reloading.
- Slanting the weapon away from the ejection port can degrade the weapon's ability to allow any debris to clear the weapon.
- Shoot only recommended ammunition.
- Discard any bad magazines.
- When correcting malfunctions or reloading, always maintain muzzle awareness (i.e., weapon pointed in a safe direction or downrange) with a straight trigger finger.

LOW- AND NO-LIGHT SHOOTING

Dealing with a determined threat in low- or no-light environments is much more complicated than one might expect. Many mistaken-identity shootings are a result of diminished vision. These situations increase the likelihood of a confrontation with a threat as your ability to perform the required combative tasks deteriorates.

It is an inescapable conclusion that in order to be able to effectively shoot in the low-light environment, we need to be able to see. We need to be able to identify friend or foe. We need to be able to determine where the threat is in order to neutralize it. Without sufficient light, we cannot be certain of our target and will most likely miss the vast majority of our targets.

Once you understand how to fight at night, you can turn darkness to an advantage. Darkness can be your friend!

The Human Eye

Since the human eye does not work as efficiently in reduced light settings as it does in full light, it is helpful to have a basic understanding of just how the eye works.

There are two types of photoreceptor cells in the retina which, because of their shapes, are called rods and cones. The retina, similar to the lens of a camera, allows in light that interacts with these light-sensitive cells.

Rods and cones contain pigments that absorb light. Nerve impulses generated by rods and cones in the retinas of the eyes travel along the optic nerves to the optic chiasma. "Mixed" impulses from both eyes pass through the optic tracts to the striate cortex at the back of the brain and end in the temporal lobe area so that right and left halves of the visual field merge.

Inside the human eye there are over 130 million rods and 7 million cones. These are arranged in such a way as to produce the best possible combination of night and day vision. Animals with high densities of rods tend to be nocturnal.

Since the rods are located on the outer portion of the retina, they are most effective for peripheral vision. Rods are sensitive enough to respond to a single photon, but together they create only one coarse, gray image, which is just adequate for seeing in poor light. Rods work best in diminished light and when the eyes scan rather than focus on an object or area. Vision in low light depends on rods.

Rods tend to show images with blurred edges. They contain a pigment called rhodopsin or "visual purple." The visual purple is what enables rods to perform well at night and allow us to have "night vision." Visual purple is chemically related to vitamin A.

Colds, headaches, fatigue, prescriptions, smoking, and alcohol negatively affect the production of visual purple. You can enhance your vision by taking keratin and vitamin E.

Normal vision is 20/20. Visual acuity drops to the 20/400–20/600 range when your eyes utilize rods to create an image in low-light conditions.

Vision in day light depends on cones. Cones are located in the central portion at the rear of the eye and work well in bright environments and enable color vision. They do not function in diminished light environments.

Cones are most important for perceiving color and sharpness in objects. Cones allow us to have great acuity and enable us to see in detail. Cones work best by looking directly at a target or area. Fine detail and color come from the cones. Unlike rods, cones work best when the eye is looking directly at an item or area. When your cones are working, the rods shut down and vice versa.

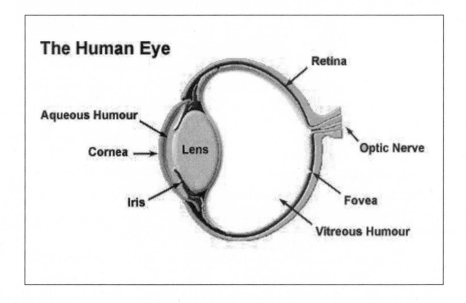

You begin to lose color vision before nautical twilight and in the low light indoor environments. You initially lose night vision by losing your ability to see colors. You lose red first, then green, then blue, and finally yellow.

The illustration on the opposite page shows a functional diagram for the rods which are spread throughout the retina, and the cones which are localized in the area of the fovea.

The eye's ability to focus peaks at age 10 and begins to decline during your mid-to-late 20s. The eye's field of view, or effective breadth of vision, begins to narrow in the late 30s. About every 13

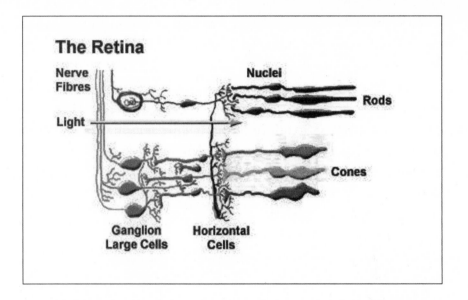

years the amount of light a person requires to see an object in low-light conditions doubles.

You need to have your night vision to be effective in low and no light. It takes at least 20–40 minutes to produce enough visual purple to enable your night vision.

Training in Low and No-Light Environments

When trying to see at night, it is best to scan an area or use "off-center vision" rather than to focus on any one item or location. Try to look at objects with your peripheral vision. By using short, abrupt, and irregular eye movements you will maximize your perception and allow fresh rod cells to be used. Try to view the item or location above or below or to the side.

Since each eye is independent and develops night vision independently, law enforcement and military often close their dominate eye when moving into and out of a lighted area to preserve some visual purple. For instance, this is a technique they would use when running from a low-light area into a well-lit area and then back into a low-light area. If one eye were not kept closed in the light, the shooter would not have any night vision at all once he went back to the diminished light area.

In the SEAL teams we always used a red lens flashlight instead of a white light to preserve night vision. A red light will enable you to see and to read but does not ruin your night vision and does not give away your position as easily as a white lens light.

At night, stay in the shadows to avoid being seen, and use whatever ambient light is available to your advantage, e.g., stars, moons, street lights.

At distances of 25 yards or more, in low or no light, your better option will probably be to avoid the fight, retreat, and take cover. A pistol fight even in daylight is difficult at 25 yards.

In low- or no-light situations, as soon as you illuminate you need to shoot, move, take cover, and/or change your profile. Your muzzle flash and/or your flashlight will give away your position and give the threat a place to shoot. As civilians or law enforcement personnel, we cannot simply shoot at a muzzle flash; but remember that the threat can and does. Your own muzzle flash will also cause temporary blindness and ruin your night vision. Muzzle flash will vary depending on your weapon and ammunition. However, it can work to your advantage. If in close proximity to the threat your muzzle flash can provide illumination for your second or multiple shots. Silver-tip ammo causes the most severe muzzle flash.

At certain times, when working in darkened buildings, you may be better off just turning on the building/house lights, than using your flashlight. This is a tactic law enforcement and military use quite often.

Knowing your natural point of aim will significantly improve your night shooting abilities. Many people tend to shoot high in the low light. When people can't see their sights they sometimes tend to raise their muzzle. To combat this, these same shooters will purposely aim lower in the darkness. The Israelis like to lower their stance in the darkness and keep their NPOA.

Light discipline is every bit as important as noise discipline. Do not give away your position by inadvertently flashing your light or making unnecessary noises.

If you do not train in low-light/no-light situations, you will never really appreciate the skills required to shoot well in diminished light. The odds of having to use defensive shooting at night are over 75 percent although most civilians, law enforcement, and many military units train mainly in the light.

Your training needs to be done by feel. Do not look at your weapon, your holster, your magazine pouch, etc. Check your weapon twice by feeling the chamber and magazine with your small finger. You may not be able to visually check the condition of your weapon if it is too dark.

The Flashlight

Since most shootings occur in low- or no-light situations, you will need a flashlight and will need to know how to shoot with it. The defensive shooter needs to be able to combine bright, operator-controlled light, with a defensive weapon if he expects to be prepared for an encounter in diminished light. Military and law enforcement personnel often carry more than one light. In the SEAL teams we always said *"one is none, two is one."* This just meant a back-up is a good plan.

You can have the flashlight mounted or not mounted on your weapon. The main disadvantage of having a light mounted on the weapon is that when you scan with the weapon, you are pointing a loaded weapon at everything you look at (Safety Rule #2).

Flashlight Shooting Techniques

Flashlights work well in a defensive environment by shining them on walls or floors to illuminate large areas. The ceilings and

Keep flashlight in an easy-to-reach position

Author utilizing the Harries Technique—the most popular flashlight technique.

walls of most residential and office buildings are either white or lightly colored. Keep in mind that with weapon mounted lights, if the shooter is illuminating a person, the muzzle is sweeping that person whether he is a threat or not. And that is a clear violation of Safety Rule #2. There are some law enforcement departments that no longer issue weapon-mounted lights for this reason alone.

All flashlight techniques (excluding those using weapon-mounted lights) require some change in stance or an unnatural grip.

- There are two categories of flashlight techniques, ("hands together" to stabilize grip or "hands apart") and about fifteen techniques in those two categories.

Harries Technique

This technique was developed in the early '70s by Mike Harries, a former Marine and member of the Southwest Pistol League with Jeff Cooper, and is the most widely taught and practiced flashlight technique.

STEPS FOR USING THE HARRIES TECHNIQUE
- Ice pick grip on the flashlight
- Thumb operates switch
- Weapon hand goes over flashlight—do not cover your hand with weapon.
- Keep elbow low for support hand holding flashlight
- Maintain wrist-to-wrist, opposing pressure with isometric tension.

The Harries technique is not a good search technique as it is only effective only in short term and is very fatiguing.

Chapman's Technique

This second most widely taught flashlight technique was developed by Ray Chapman, the first world champion of the sport of practical shooting and founder of the Chapman Academy of Practical Shooting.

STEPS FOR USING THE CHAPMAN TECHNIQUE
* Sword grip
* Hold flashlight along side of pistol.
* Thumb and forefinger encircle the light; other three fingers grip shooting hand.

Rogers Technique

This non-fatiguing technique was developed by Bill Rogers, a former FBI Agent and police instructor, and a world ranked IPSC shooter with over 40 years of shooting competition experience.

STEPS FOR USING THE ROGERS TECHNIQUE
* It requires a Sure Fire-type light with a rear-mounted pressure switch.
* Hold light between index and middle finger.
* Back of flashlight touches palm or heel of support hand.
* Gun is held in a normal grip, palm pressure from support hand activates light.

Ayoob Technique (modified version of Chapman's style)

Massad Ayoob developed this technique. He is the director of the Lethal Force Institute whose shooting skills have won him numerous local, state, regional, and national titles. He is one of the first to have earned a four-gun master rating in IDPA and is recognized as one of the best firearms instructors in the country. Ayoob's technique is good for a quick, sudden response to a threat, but is not suited for room searching. It is not a natural position, but it is easy to assume.

STEPS FOR USING THE AYOOB TECHNIQUE
* Sword grip

Author utilizing the Rogers Technique

- Lightly supported
- Bring both hands to an approximate isosceles position and end with both thumbs touching to create isometric tension that steadies the weapon.
- Other common flashlight techniques and steps for use include:

FBI Technique
- Sword or ice pick grip
- The oldest flashlight technique

Author utilizing the FBI Technique

- Known as the "misaligned technique"
- Eliminates "hand confusion"
- A relaxed technique good for room clearing
- Holding the light away from your body is disorienting from the assailant's point of view. It also allows the shooter to scan without covering with a loaded weapon and to move light to further confuse the threat.

Neck Technique

- Works with large and small flashlights alike
- Works well with those possessing varying switch configurations
- Provides simultaneous illumination of sights and the threat
- Flashlight can easily be used as a striking tool from this position
- Can be used with an injured arm or hand
- A disadvantage is that it draws fire toward the shooter's head
- Hold the flashlight in an ice pick grip against the jaw/neck juncture below the ear

Hargreaves Technique (British Army Operator):

- Flashlight held in palm of hand, weak hand is under the pistol.
- Requires the use of gross motor skills only.

Keller Technique (Georgia State Law Enforcement Trooper):

- A modification of the Harries technique
- Sword grip
- Shooting hand below support hand

Note: When law enforcement or military enter a building where the lights are off, one technique is to simply turn the lights on. This sounds very rudimentary, but for years law enforcement and military personnel used darkness as an advantage and would keep building lights off.

Author utilizing the Neck Technique

Weapon-Mounted Lights

Advantages:

- Leave both hands free to handle weapon
- Gives instant availability and control of light whenever you have your weapon in your hand, without degrading your ability to shoot
- Gives the ability to switch the light on and off instantly, without changing your grip on the weapon

Disadvantage:

- Use of weapon-mounted lights requires that you either violate Safety Rule #2 and search with the weapon, or use a light-colored ceiling or wall to reflect light into the area that you wish to illuminate.

Tips:

- Link the non-gun-hand wrist with a flashlight lanyard. So if you drop your flashlight, have to reload, or clear malfunctions, you will not lose your flashlight. If you do not have a lanyard on your flashlight, place it under your shooting arm with the light turned off and facing toward the rear when performing malfunction clearing procedures and reloads. In the event your light is inadvertently switched on, at least it will be behind you and won't completely illuminate you or your actions.
- Flashlights offer plenty of benefits other than giving the shooter the capability of seeing in the dark.
- You always need a light when you carry a weapon (for searches, trunks, cellars, attics, loss of power, night shooting, etc.).
- You can use a strong light by directing it into the threat's eyes, momentary blinding and disorienting him. A high-intensity light can actually force a threat to snap his head back when the main part of the beam strikes his eyes. This may give you time to draw and take cover, if you haven't already done so.
- A flashlight may allow you to observe a threat's hands.

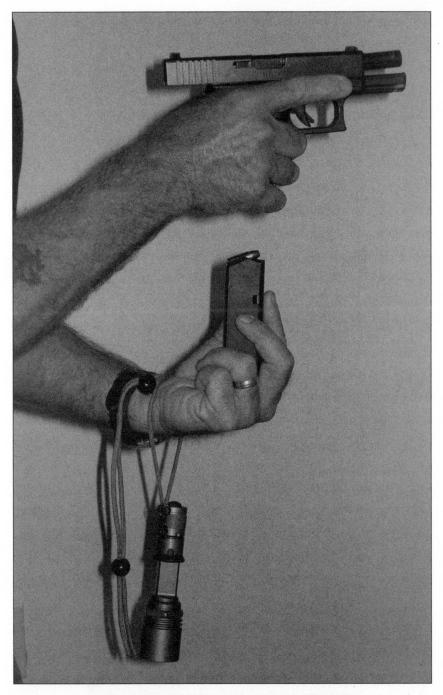

Author conducting a reload with a lanyard on flashlight

- You can use your flashlight to direct movement.
- You can intentionally illuminate your position.
- A flashlight can be used as a "legal" weapon. Many shooters attach a tactical impact device to the lens to make it a very effective weapon.
- A flashlight next to your weapon can illuminate your sights.
- Your light does not have to be directly on a target to illuminate the target.
- Using a flashlight takes practice; and dry practice is very effective in mastering these techniques.
- Whenever you illuminate, you should move since you may have given away your position. "Illuminate, shoot, move."
- Protect your flashlight and provide it with a better gripping surface with rubber, e.g., bike inner tube, rubber bands, etc. Disadvantages of using a flashlight:
- The use of a light can also give away your position. The newer flashlights are very powerful and create a lot of light "spillover," which illuminates the user.
- Light takes away your night vision.

Night Sights

Normal sights are typically not visible in diminished light. Julio Santiago, a former law enforcement agent, introduced the luminous tritium "night sights" in the late 1980s. After Julio put the tritium on his weapon and established night sights, he was contacted by the FBI to conduct night sight shooting tests for the FBI. These tests established instant credibility for his new concept and before long the night sight was adopted by the weapons community.

A problem with night sights is if you simply line up three night sights and fire, you could shoot with the sights off target. With three similar glowing dots, you could get the front sight cocked to the side of the rear sight sufficiently to misread a proper alignment when your sights are really not aligned at all. There are several options to correct this problem, including brighter dots on the front, bars on the rear or different colors on the rear.

Lasers

Advantages:

- Dramatically increase one's ability to shoot accurately and effectively in low-light situations.
- They are widely recognized for their intimidation or deterrent value, similar to that of racking of a shotgun. Some threats have even given up when they saw the red dot on their chest.
- Pulsating beam attracts the target's attention more so than a steady beam.
- They do not replace your weapon's conventional sights, but rather augment them.
- Lasers allow you to shoot with both eyes open.
- Many lasers are protected since they are installed inside of the weapon.
- Most lasers allow for the use of any holster.

The laser may not be visible on your target in bright light or in a smoky, dusty, or foggy environment. In addition, the reflection off the particles in such an environment may trace a line straight back to the weapon, giving away your location. And under stress, in the dark, you may unintentionally squeeze your laser switch prematurely or fail to relax your grip on it while moving, also revealing your location.

Lasers work well in certain situations. For instance, if you have been incapacitated to the point that you cannot lift the gun to the sighting plane, a laser sight will allow you to fire a shot with more precision than merely pointing the weapon; however it must be remembered that unlike a flashlight, a laser does not illuminate targets.

If you choose to equip your weapon with a laser, don't substitute the laser for training with the conventional sights. Training with the sights conditions you to bring the gun to the same sighting plane every time that you shoot.

Disadvantages:

- The use of a laser requires a great deal of practice, and some models require two hands to manually work the on/off switch.
- There is an accepted "wobble zone" for lasers that still yields results, but you must have the trigger manipulation down.

Aimpoints

The major benefit of Aimpoint sights is they allow you to shoot with both eyes open, like a laser. An Aimpoint is a bright sharp dot that can be turned down to invisible for use with night vision devices. Aimpoints can last for up to 10,000 hours on a battery and they allow for a quicker shot than aligning the front and rear sights. They are parallax free (parallax occurs when the aiming point—red dot/cross hair—moves on the target when the shooter moves his/her head). If your head is not lined up exactly as you sighted in your weapon, your round will not hit the point of aim.

Batteries

A flashlight is worthless without dependable and effective battery. When selecting your batteries it may be important to note that power is measured in watts, and the power delivered by the battery is found by multiplying the battery's voltage by the amperes that the battery delivers to the light source.

The amount of electrical energy stored by the battery is best specified in watt-hours, although battery manufacturers always rate their batteries in ampere-hours.

The biggest difference in a lithium battery over an alkaline battery is that lithium batteries can deliver more than four times more watts.

Your choice of batteries determines the size and weight of your flashlight and your operating cost. Batteries can be primary or rechargeable, but remember that a battery's self-discharge rate has a significant effect on its practical reliability.

Lithium Batteries

Lithium batteries are 30 percent shorter and lighter than alkaline batteries and have a ten-year shelf life as compared to three to four years. Lithium batteries are expensive and only have a one-hour life span, but they are the brightest. As such, these batteries are for target ID and not for prolonged use, e.g., searching.

Lithium batteries cannot only deliver more power (in watts), but they do so without excessive voltage decline. They store up to 50 percent more useable energy than AA alkaline batteries, and operate at temperatures much lower than alkaline batteries.

Alkaline Batteries

Alkaline batteries are serviceable, but they have one main drawback: They cannot deliver high wattage without their voltage draining sharply.

Rechargeable Batteries

Rechargeable batteries are normally nickel-cadmium (ni-cad) and are bigger and heavier than lithium batteries. Still, they tend to be less expensive in the long run.

CONCEALED CARRY AND HOLSTERS

"I am concerned for the security of our great Nation; not so much because of any threat from without, but because of the insidious forces working from within."
— General Douglas MacArthur

Concealed Carry

Any concealed carry method has two basic requirements, it must conceal the weapon and must not impede your ability to draw the weapon quickly. There is a trade-off between concealment and accessibility—the better the concealment, the worse the accessibility and vice versa.

Dark colors and clothing with "busy" patterns generally "print" a weapon less than light colors. ("Printing" occurs when the outline of the weapon is visible through the clothing.) And heavier or thicker clothing tends to conceal a weapon better than thinner clothing.

Do not wear something that is out of season or out of style because it will draw attention. For example, the popular safari/

photojournalist vests, or as they call them overseas, the "CIA-CNN" vests, offer concealment for most belt holsters, but in many places around the world they are very obvious.

As for accessibility, when you draw a concealed weapon, you go through the same three stages as you do with open carry: 1) Grip, 2) Ready, and 3) Up. The exact way you perform each of these steps depends on where the weapon is concealed and how the hand that retrieves it is positioned.

Holster Selection

A holster must secure the weapon and release it easily when you want it. Unfortunately many of the concealment holsters do not provide these qualities.

Some shooters strongly believe that a handgun should be carried in an open-top holster for faster draw. But if you take a fall or have to run and jump over obstacles, you need your weapon to remain in the holster. This is especially relevant if the fall, run, or jump has taken place in the dark, in the woods, on a hillside, beside a body of water, or in the snow or mud.

Holsters can be constructed from either leather, ballistic nylon, Kydex, or composite material. Leather does not hold up as well in wet, rainy, or jungle climates as some of the polymer (like Kydex) and ballistic nylon holsters. These synthetic materials are more resistant to water and heat and are also usually quite a bit cheaper than leather. If you do use a leather holster, do not store your weapon in it over a long period of time. The materials used in some of the leathers can cause corrosion problems to the finish of the weapon.

Kydex is an extremely tough, rigid thermoplastic that can be molded into holsters and accessories. It is relatively inexpensive; durable and easily cleaned; lightweight; withstands extreme temperatures; and has excellent retention characteristics. However, because Kydex holsters are so rigid, they may be more uncomfortable than inside the waistband (IWB) leather holsters.

When choosing a holster, regardless of the material, ensure it is made to fit your specific type of weapon.

Thumb Breaks

Thumb breaks are offered on many belt, shoulder, and ankle holsters. A thumb break is a strap that fastens around the weapon to keep it securely in the holster while still allowing quick access.

Thumb breaks are different from the traditional holster retaining straps in that the fastener is located on the dominant-hand thumb side of the holster. This allows the thumb break to be unfastened with the dominant-hand thumb as the hand grips the weapon to draw it from the holster. Thumb breaks are much quicker to draw from than a holster with traditional retaining straps, and they offer the same service of keeping the weapon from accidentally falling out of the holster.

Thumb breaks are slightly slower to draw from than open-top holsters, but with practice this difference can be reduced to tenths of a second. Some thumb breaks are difficult to "break" with the support hand in the event the dominant hand is injured or otherwise out of use, however.

Sight Rails

Sight rails are pieces of material (usually leather, plastic, or rubber) stitched or molded into the holster to form a "channel" the length of the holster around the front sight of the gun.

Sight rails are intended to keep the front sight from snagging the holster as the weapon is holstered or drawn. Snagging the sights can slow down the draw and/or tear pieces of material out of the holster and deposit them on your front sight, leaving an obscured front sight.

Holsters that do not have sight rails are typically made in such a way that a channel is formed around the front sight for the entire length of the holster. This channel serves the same purpose as sight rails.

It is important to break in a new holster thoroughly on the range or at home before betting your life on it. Leather holsters, in particular, require a solid break-in period. Some custom leather holsters fit so snugly when new that they require more than a hundred practice draws before they are broken in enough to carry.

Hackaworth Rip

Ken Hackaworth developed a clearing method called the Hackaworth Rip, our standard draw technique. It is one of the most

common and preferred methods of concealment if the holster is worn on the strong side with a garment covering the weapon.

With your support hand, grab the bottom of the concealing material, and swiftly lift it up toward the support hand side. You may also want to bend from the hips away from your weapon making for quicker access. While simple to use, this technique does not work well

Concealed carry— closed garment

when wearing long concealing or tight materials, or if your support hand is occupied with another task, such as holding a flashlight or deflecting the threat's attack.

The Belt

A commonly overlooked component of belt holsters is the belt itself. The importance of a good holster belt for belt carry cannot be stressed enough. A good belt that properly fits your holster will keep the weapon secured, even during physical activities such as running or jumping.

You want your weapon to remain in exactly the same place on your body during physical activity so that when you reach for it, it will be exactly where you expect it to be. If your weapon shifts position during movement, it can cause you to lose precious seconds when drawing.

And, of course, you want to retain the weapon on your person. A flimsy belt will not hold the holster in place, and this can cause concealment problems as well as the problem of retaining the weapon.

The ideal holster belt for concealed carry will provide good vertical and tensional strength without being too wide. This usually means a leather belt, since most fabric belts have poor lateral strength. The belt may need to be an inch or two longer than your normal size belt when not carrying a holster.

Belt Holsters

Belt holsters are the most traditional holsters for handguns. The choice of a belt holster involves many factors: body shape, weapon, weather, activities, and clothing.

Belt holsters can be broken down into two basic categories: those that are worn inside the waist band (IWB) and those that are worn outside of the waist band (OWB).

IWB HOLSTERS

IWB holsters are worn with the grip of the handgun remaining above the belt. Since the grip is all that remains above the belt, this is the hardest and most critical part of the weapon to conceal with an IWB holster. A weapon with a short, thin, rounded grip conceals well in an IWB holster. Grips with sharp edges tend to print more than grips with rounded edges.

A revolver is typically less comfortable for IWB carry because the cylinder is relatively thick and tends to dig into your side in an IWB holster. A 1911 is much more comfortable in an IWB holster than a snub-nose .38 Special.

Most IWB holsters are worn on the strong side slightly behind the hip and some are worn cross-draw or farther back on the strong side near the kidney area.

If wearing a coat, vest or jacket, carry some object of slight weight (such as fishing weights) in the strong side pocket. This will give the garment some momentum so that once it is swept out of the way during the draw it will clear the holster and allow the wearer to draw without fumbling with it while finding the grip.

Advantages:
- IWB holsters are among the most concealable and versatile of all holsters.
- IWB holsters can often be concealed simply with an untucked shirt, while other belt holsters usually require a jacket or vest for effective concealment.
- With the right combination of holster, body type, handgun, and clothing, a surprisingly large handgun can be concealed in the waistband effectively and comfortably.

Disadvantages:
- IWB holsters are not as comfortable as most OWB holsters.
- The mouth of many IWB holsters collapses after the weapon is drawn, making it more difficult to re-holster.
- Your pants will need to be at least one or two inches larger in the waist than normal especially if you also wear an IWB magazine pouch.
- An IWB holster exposes your weapon to perspiration since it is carried close to the body. Because of this, a weapon with a corrosion-resistant finish may be preferable to a plain blued finish for IWB carry.

- A short-barreled gun does not fit well in an IWB holster since the weapon becomes somewhat top-heavy.

Holsterless IWB

The holsterless IWB carry method is designed for revolvers, but without actually using a holster. This method is fairly comfortable, inexpensive, and is ideal for warm weather use. Weapons can be effectively concealed with pants or shorts and an untucked shirt, provided that the shirt has a sufficiently long tail. The disadvantage of the holsterless IWB carry method is that it is not as secure during physical activities as when using a holster.

"Below-the-Waistband" IWB Holsters

With these types of holsters the entire weapon is concealed beneath the waistband. They are slower to draw from than most belt holsters and virtually require you to be standing in order to draw the weapon. Since these holsters suspend the weapon below the belt line, they do not take advantage of natural body contours of some body types.

OWB Holsters

The primary advantages with an outside-the-pants holster are comfort and accessibility. Disadvantages include: These holsters take a little more effort to conceal than the IWB holsters; they typically require an outer garment such as a sweater, jacket, or vest for concealment, so they are not quite as versatile as IWB holsters; and because some part of all OWB holsters extends below the belt, they require a longer concealing garment than the IWB holsters.

Pancake/Scabbard Holsters

Pancake and scabbard holsters are types of OWB holsters and are virtually identical in design. Pancake holsters typically have the belt slots on either side of the holster to allow the holster to be drawn in close to the body, while scabbard holsters may have only one belt slot.

They are offered with a variety of options: thumb breaks, open tops, various cants, and open or covered muzzle designs.

Advantages:
- They can be concealed by a shorter outer garment.
- Many pancake holsters are shaped so they fit the contours of the body.
- They are very comfortable.
- They allow a full range of motion
- They provide a firm anchor for your handgun.

Concealed carry—open garment

- They allow for one of the fastest draws of any concealment holster.

Disadvantages:
- This holster makes the weapon top-heavy.

CROSS-DRAW HOLSTER

This holster is worn on the support-side hip and is a good choice for someone who spends a lot of time in a vehicle. Since it usually is slightly forward from the actual side of the hip, it is more difficult to conceal with a coat (the bulge tends to protrude a bit), but if you keep one button fastened on the coat, it works without interfering with accessibility.

BELT SLIDES

Most belt slides are just a slide or loop that the belt is threaded through. The weapon is either OWB and through the slide or between the belt and trousers and through the slide. Many belt slides are not easily identified as holsters, which may be desirable for people who want to wear their holster all the time in case the need arises to carry their gun. Disadvantages of using this type of holster include: They do not always adequately secure the weapon; the front sights sometimes snag on the belt slide since the barrel is "unguided" during the first few inches of the draw, so and if the slide is not fitted properly to the weapon, it can fall out of the holster.

PADDLE HOLSTERS

Paddle holsters have a thin, paddle-shaped piece of material attached to a traditional-looking OWB holster. The "paddle," which may be constructed of leather, plastic, or some other combination of materials, is inserted into the waistband. The paddle material is usually flexible so that it conforms to the shape of the shooter's hip. This paddle is supposed to keep the holster securely positioned so that it will not shift.

Advantages:
- They are available with different cants and carrying heights.
- They can be donned and removed easily.
- They are more comfortable than an IWB holster since only a thin paddle is in the pants versus the entire gun.
- They can be removed without taking off the belt.
- They do not always require a belt.

Disadvantages:

- They are more difficult to conceal than the IWB holster
- Often, when you draw, the holster stays attached to the weapon, which can be a catastrophic disadvantage.

SMALL-OF-THE-BACK HOLSTERS (SOB)

The SOB holster sits in a horizontal position on the belt in the middle of the back.

Advantages:

- These are very popular with shooters who do a lot of standing and walking, versus sitting in vehicles.
- They are an excellent choice for those who ride motorcycles, ATVs, bicycles, or horses, since these activities do not require you to sit with your back against anything.
- They do not get in the way as much as other OWB holsters when bending at the waist.
- They do not require as long an outer garment for concealment as the other OWB holsters.

CROSS-DRAW BELT HOLSTERS

Note: Many of the above-mentioned OWB holsters may be worn in a cross-draw fashion. But beware that unless the draw is executed perfectly, the muzzle of the weapon can sweep part of the shooter's body (Safety Rule #2) or innocent parties nearby.

Advantages:

- Allow for a faster draw than the other type of belt holsters
- Allow for easy access to your weapon, which is particularly advantageous in a vehicle
- When wearing a jacket or vest for concealment, you can simply reach into the garment through the front to access the weapon.

- Allow the quickest and easiest access of any belt holster with the support hand in the event that the dominant hand is immobile or disabled

Disadvantages:
- The weapon is positioned so that it can be easily grabbed by a threat.
- It nearly always requires an outer garment for concealment. Because the shape of the body forward of the hip prevents the weapon from being pulled in close against the body, an un-tucked shirt often will not adequately conceal even an IWB cross-draw holster.
- If a suit coat is worn to conceal a cross-draw holster, it must remain buttoned for effective concealment. However, because of the position of the holster, it is often possible to draw the weapon by reaching in without having to unbutton the coat.

Shoulder, Below-the-Knee, and Pocket Holsters

Shoulder Holsters

There are many types of shoulder holsters, and all are suspended by at least one strap that passes over one or both shoulders for support. Most shoulder holster harnesses are designed in a figure-eight pattern with the center of the harness sitting on the top part of the back and shoulders. The weapon is carried under the support arm so that it can be drawn with the dominant hand.

Advantages:
- The ability to draw while seated. This makes a shoulder holster useful in a vehicle.
- They are practical for cold-weather clothing. The weapon in a shoulder holster can be reached nonchalantly. An outer garment that is unfastened down to the midchest level will still provide

ready access to the weapon; this is not the case with a belt holster since the coat must be swept away to access the gun.

- Spare magazines, speed loaders, or other accessories can be attached to the harness.
- Can be easily weight balanced when a double magazine case is worn under the dominant arm
- They distribute the weight of the weapon and the accessories over the shoulders, versus having the weight concentrated in one small area.
- The harness may also be further secured via a "tie-down," which is a strap that secures the holster harness to the belt.
- The weapon may be carried horizontally, vertically, or canted, depending upon the style of holster and the shooter's preference.
- Most holsters can be adjusted to fit a variety of body sizes.
- The most concealable and the fastest drawing shoulder holsters carry the weapon nearly horizontal with a slight muzzle-up cant. This allows the weapon to be drawn smoothly and in a natural fashion.

Disadvantages:
- They require a sleeved outer garment for concealment since the shoulder holster harness can be seen through the arm openings.
- Even when wearing a coat, shoulder holsters are often visible when you bend forward, since the concealing garment has a tendency to open.
- A weapon carried in a shoulder holster is vulnerable to being snatched by a threat.
- They are hard to conceal on a thin person.
- The harness must be concealed as well as the holster.
- Shoulder holster adjustments are somewhat difficult to make alone, though a well-adjusted shoulder rig will substantially improve comfort and concealability. If not adjusted properly, the

X in the harness will flex and be visible through your concealing garment during some movements.

- A quality shoulder holster is significantly more expensive than a belt holster of the same quality.
- Horizontal shoulder holsters inherently violate Safety Rule #2: "Never let your muzzle cover anything you are not willing to destroy." If you are carrying in a horizontal shoulder holster, your muzzle can sweep anything behind you. As with cross-draw carry, with some shoulder holsters it is easy to sweep part of your body with the muzzle during the draw or holstering.

BELOW-THE-KNEE HOLSTERS

There are two basic kinds of below-the-knee leg holsters, those that are carried around the upper portion of the calf and those that are worn around the ankle.

Most ankle holsters are worn on the inside of the non-dominant-side leg so they can be reached more easily with the dominant hand and when worn in position they are not susceptible to bumping into something.

They are made of leather, ballistic nylon, or an elasticized fabric. Many ankle holsters are made with a padded backing for comfort. One way to improve ankle holster concealment is to tuck the lower portion of the holster into your sock. This way, even if the cuff of the pants slides up, the holster will not be apparent.

Advantages:
- The ankle holster offers appreciably faster access than the calf holster.
- They are easily accessible when seated, which works well in a vehicle.
- The weapon can be reached when lying flat on your back. Many lives have been saved when a shooter being was able to reach his ankle rig while wrestling with a threat. A belt or shoulder holster

may not be reached easily if your body weight and/or the weight of a threat is on top of the weapon.

- The weapon can be reached with either the dominant or non-dominant hand.
- If there is a chance you may be hugged, an ankle holster will provide more discretion than most forms of concealed carry. Belt, shoulder and even pocket holsters may be discovered easily during an embrace.

Concealed carry draw from the ankle holster

Disadvantages:

- They are generally slower to draw from than any of the belt holsters.
- It is difficult to reach your weapon in an ankle rig while you are standing unless you are able to place your leg on an object such as a car bumper.
- Ankle and calf holsters require long pants, so they are often not appropriate for extremely hot weather. Even with flared trouser legs, a full-sized handgun cannot be carried in an ankle or calf holster discretely, so you are limited to smaller weapons. Because of their size limitation, however, these holsters are a good choice for secondary weapons.
- Since ankle rigs are close to the ground the weapon can pick up a lot of dirt, grime, water or snow.

POCKET HOLSTERS

There are three basic types of pocket holsters: pants pocket holsters; rear pants pocket or wallet holsters; and coat or vest pocket holsters.

Advantages:

- Many smaller weapons can be carried in pockets inconspicuously.
- If the clothing worn is minimal, a pocket holster can be an excellent option.
- Very comfortable
- Very convenient
- Relatively inexpensive
- Generally speaking, the weapon can be easy to access without looking too conspicuous.
- The tactical advantage of using a front, wallet or coat-pocket holster is that you can nonchalantly put your hand in your pocket as though you are reaching for your cell phone or wallet.

This allows you to index and achieve a firing grip without ever exposing your weapon.

- With a pocket holster, you have the ability to point and fire a handgun through the concealing garment's pocket if necessary.

Disadvantages:
- In some states, it is illegal to carry a weapon in a pocket without a holster even if you have a concealed carry permit.
- The weapon may not be properly positioned for drawing from the pocket.
- The weapon may print through the pocket.
- The weapon can get dirty from being carried loose in the pocket.
- Does not afford for a fast draw.
- The biggest disadvantage is the size of the weapon that can be carried in a pocket. Also, front pants pocket holsters may violate Safety Rule #2. When you are seated normally, your thigh is roughly horizontal. Any gun carried in your front pants pocket may be horizontal too, with the muzzle covering the area in front of you.

Accessory Holsters

Regardless of the clothes you wear, there is an accessory holster that can enable you to conceal a handgun under virtually any circumstance. Following are some examples:

Butt Packs

One of the most common accessory holsters is the butt (or fanny) pack. These are commonly used by hikers, climbers, cyclists, skiers, and tourists. They are small, lightweight, and easily put on or removed. They provide a means for carrying a weapon, spare ammo, and other small items while keeping hands free for other tasks.

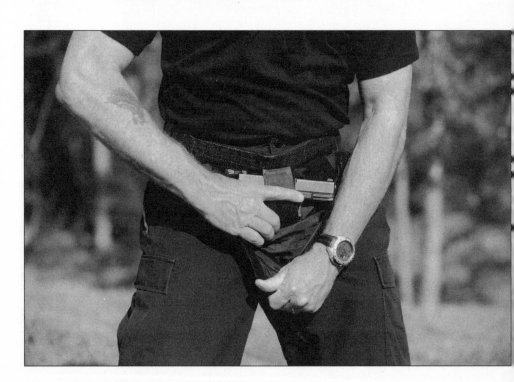

Concealed carry drawn from the butt pack

For a right-handed person, the pack is generally worn in front of the left hip. This allows you to open the pack with your support hand and draw the weapon with your dominant hand.

Most packs are made of ballistic nylon, but models are also available in leather. The typical butt pack has a strap that fastens around the waist with a simple three-pronged clip. These straps can be clipped on quickly, but they can also be unclipped and cut easily and snatched by an experienced thief. My butt pack has a steel wire cable that runs through the strap so it cannot be cut off my waist.

Advantages:
* Butt packs offer shooters of all body types an opportunity to carry a full-sized handgun without clothing restrictions.

- Because regular butt packs are so popular, these holsters are not very conspicuous (except to those "in the know").
- Many of these packs have a separate compartment for the weapon and another compartment for other items, e.g., flashlight, cell phone, spare ammo.
- They come in a variety of sizes to fit most handguns.
- The holster compartment of most packs is backed with a semi-rigid material that provides a firm foundation for the weapon.
- They do not require a concealing outer garment; thus, they can be worn in warm weather without excessive clothing.
- They can be strapped on or removed easily and quickly.
- They blend in when worn in tourist areas.
- Because they allow the weapon to be carried forward of the hip, butt pack holsters are good for driving or other seated activities.
- The excellent weight distribution of most butt packs provides comfort during extended carry.
- They are quite versatile, expanding your concealed carry options.
- They are comfortable and especially convenient when engaged in moderately active physical activities, such as hiking and biking.

Disadvantages:
- They can be stolen fairly easily, either by unfastening the strap buckle or by cutting the strap.
- They cannot be used as a single all-purpose concealed carry holster because they are not socially appropriate for all occasions.
- They are not especially good for cold weather carry, since a coat or jacket worn over the pack makes drawing difficult.
- Because of the popularity of butt pack holsters, they are no longer a secret. If you have a working knowledge of the various types of butt pack holsters, it is not difficult to spot the ones that are actually holsters.

Belt-Case Holsters

Similar to butt pack holsters, camera case or belt case holsters offer additional versatility. A camera case holster either clips onto the belt, has belt loops, or both. These cases come in different sizes to accommodate handguns of all sizes. These belt case holsters have their openings fastened either with Velcro or a dual zipper arrangement, similar to a butt pack holster.

Advantage:
- Camera case holsters have the advantage of looking just like belt camera cases, which makes them perfect for tourist areas or other events where cameras are widely used.

Disadvantages:
- Since they look like camera cases, they are limited in their applications. If the situation is not appropriate for a camera, then a camera case holster would be conspicuous.
- Cameras are often the target of thieves and muggers, so a camera case holster may draw undesirable attention.

Portfolio/Briefcase Holsters

Portfolio holsters look like conventional over-the-shoulder carry bags. They are made from a variety of materials, including ballistic nylon, leather, and canvas. Most portfolio holsters have a separate compartment for the weapon.

Some of the portfolios with the body armor compartment have a strap that can be placed around the neck so the portfolio can actually be worn as makeshift body armor after the weapon has been drawn from the portfolio holster.

Advantages:
- Appropriate for men and women

- Can accommodate nearly any size handgun, as well as spare magazines or speed loaders
- Are widely used by the general public, so a portfolio holster offers excellent concealment

Disadvantages:
- Not a good choice for an all-purpose holster since the weapon is carried in the portfolio and not actually on your body for easy access

Day Planner Holsters

These holsters look like generic day planner notebooks. When the notebook is opened, it unfolds to reveal a holster.

This holster has most of the same advantages and disadvantages of the portfolio holster.

Advantages:
- Many professional men and women keep their day planners with them all day, so this holster would not be out of place in most urban areas during business hours.
- Many day planner holsters will accommodate most any size handgun.

Disadvantages:
- They require at least one hand for carrying at all times.
- They are more apt to be laid down to free the hands for some other task, which makes the weapon in the day planner holster more likely to fall into the wrong hands.

Bellyband Holsters

There are several different types of under-the-shirt/coat elastic band (or "bellyband") holsters. Most types are constructed of elastic bands that wrap around the waist or chest and are fastened with

Velcro. A pocket that holds the handgun is sewn into the band. With chest bellybands, the handgun is carried under the support arm. With the waist bellybands, the handgun may be carried in the middle of the waist or to one side.

Advantages:
- Available in a variety of sizes
- They can be worn under a tucked-in shirt without sacrificing concealment.
- They may be worn outside of the shirt and under a zipped or buttoned lightweight jacket, but this configuration requires that you keep the jacket buttoned.
- Revolvers with small grips tend to conceal best.
- They are as easily accessed when seated as when standing.

Disadvantages:
- When they are worn under a shirt, it is difficult to draw.
- The size of the concealed handgun is limited.
- Accessing the weapon is a relatively slow process.

Thunderwear Holsters

This holster is actually worn over the underwear and under the pants. It is basically just a pouch with a waist strap. The strap fastens around the waist and the pouch is positioned directly under the torso.

Advantages:
- Can accommodate a medium-sized handgun and a spare magazine
- They come in various sizes.
- They come in both left- and right-handed designs.
- Semis work the best since they typically have a slimmer profile.
- They are quite comfortable and offer good concealment.

- They do not require a belt.
- They allow for concealed carry with a shirt that is tucked into pants.

Disadvantages:
- The weapon can be difficult to access when seated.
- Men are required to use a booth, rather than a urinal, in public restrooms to prevent unwanted attention.
- Many shooters, understandably, have issues with carrying a loaded weapon adjacent to their genitals.
- It often takes two hands to draw the gun and acquire a firing grip.

Jacket and Vest Holsters

There are several garments on the market that have hidden pockets that serve as holsters. The weapon can be accessed by reaching across the chest into the pocket, a motion similar to accessing a shoulder holster.

Advantages:
- Offer exceptional concealment
- A good alternative to a large pocketed overcoat that is typically used to carry a full-sized handgun
- Can be easily counter balanced
- You can take the jacket off and hang it over the back of your chair and still not expose your handgun.
- Even when the wind blows your jacket open, the weapon remains concealed.

Disadvantages:
- Relatively slow access to the weapon
- The weapon tends to shift position in the large holster pocket.
- Not good for warm weather, since the jacket is the holster

Photojournalist "CIA-CNN" Vests

Advantages:
- These vests offer good concealment; they are baggy and have many pockets and flaps that cover any bulges that your weapon may make.
- They are much cooler to wear in warm weather than a jacket or other sleeved garment.
- Some of these vests may contain soft body armor.

Disadvantage:
- Many people, especially overseas, still use the safari/photojournalist vest. In my opinion, when you see someone wearing this type of vest, he or she is carrying a concealed weapon.

Other Miscellaneous Carry

There are countless other modes of concealed carry, and many do not even use holsters. Small weapons may be concealed in custom boot holsters, in the palm of one hand under a pair of gloves or mittens, or carried in the bib pocket of overalls.

Concealed Carry for Women

The anatomical differences between men and women must be considered when choosing women's concealment holsters. Women tend to be higher-waisted—their torsos make up a smaller fraction of their total height—they are generally shorter, and many tend to be hourglass shaped. For these reasons, women experience many problems when they try to wear concealed carry holsters designed for men.

Women's Belt Holsters

Since women often do not wear belts, the paddle holster is a good choice for many women. These holsters do not always require a belt, so they can be worn with a skirt or pants.

Holster Purses

Advantages:
- One of the most hassle-free modes of concealed carry for any size handgun
- Most holster purses are designed with a separate compartment for the weapon, usually accessible through a zipper or a Velcro-type closure that looks like a seam on the purse.
- A large handgun can be concealed effectively by a small woman who could not conceal the same gun in a conventional holster.
- A purse is appropriate for many occasions and the chance of one being recognized as a holster purse is slim.
- The weapon may be pointed and fired through the purse if necessary.

Disadvantages:
- Often, many additional items, other than the weapon, are carried loose in the purse, which causes difficulties in rapidly acquiring a good grip.
- A loose weapon is subject to being inadvertently revealed any time the purse is opened in public.
- A loose weapon is exposed to debris/lint from the purse that may cause functional reliability problems.
- Since it is not worn on the body, it can be separated from the shooter.
- Holster purses offer relatively slow access to the weapon.

Note: Backpacks are good alternatives for purses since they allow for hands-free carry when needed, though the gun is not as accessible.

PURSE/BRIEFCASE INSERTS

Purse/briefcase inserts are also available. They typically are designed to snap or Velcro into a purse or briefcase. The actual insert functions like a snap-in holster.

Advantages:

- The same insert can be used in a variety of purses and brief-cases.
- These offer many of the same advantages as holster purses although the weapon is not loose.
- They're relatively inexpensive.

Disadvantages:

- Poor accessibility
- A firing grip cannot always be obtained nonchalantly with an insert, because the insert is carried inside the purse.
- Inserts also have many of the same disadvantages as carrying a weapon loose in a conventional purse.
- The weapon is likely to be exposed inadvertently when the purse is opened in public.

Thigh Holsters

Thigh holsters consist of a holster band worn around the thigh and a waist belt that has a strap connecting to the holster band. The waist belt is designed to help support the weight of the weapon and the holster band via the connecting strap. This type holster is best used with small to medium weapons.

Shooting Maxims

"Carrying a loaded gun with the ability and will to use it is not a casual fling meant to bring some excitement into your boring life. It is an all-embracing lifestyle and must take precedence over your respect for law, your fear of social criticism, your love of humanity, your wardrobe, and your drinking habits."

— Anonymous

"Let your gun be your constant companion on your walks."

—Thomas Jefferson

Advantages:
- Most effectively concealed with a fairly loose skirt or dress
- Offer good concealment with the proper clothing

Disadvantages:
- Similar to ankle and calf holsters in that some people have difficulty getting accustomed to the additional weight of a weapon on one leg, though this problem is not as severe as with ankle or calf holsters because the weight is further up the leg.
- Many women find them to be uncomfortable
- Access to the thigh holster is slow and awkward.
- The weapon is difficult to access when seated.

LEARNING STYLES

No matter what you're learning, different people teach in different ways, and different weapons and tactics instructors all have their own way of teaching. In this chapter I hope to point out there is often more than one way to train and teach marksmanship and tactics and it is up to you to choose the way that works best for you.

A weapons and tactics instructor needs to move way beyond just teaching basic shooting skills to the defensive shooter. There's a significant difference between training that builds basic or advanced shooting skills on a range and training that builds tactical proficiency. Both types of training are necessary, but simply teaching shooting skills provides behavioral routines that are often not at all connected to real life scenarios.

As strange as it may sound, a novice shooter who has only been taught basic marksmanship on a range may simply stand in front of

Training others can be very rewarding. Many women tend to be natural shooters and very quick learners.

a real world threat, draw, shoot, break, and scan and then wait for the next command. If the trainee shoots well and if the threat's central nervous system is compromised, or some large organs and/or blood vessels have been ruptured, then all may turn out well.

However, if the threat is not immediately neutralized, then the shooter could very well wind up being shot while subconsciously waiting for the next command.

Many instructors tend to teach in the learning style that they favor and share what works best for them, rather than what works best for the student. The result is that students with the same learning style often learn very quickly, and students with different learning styles tend to learn poorly or not at all.

People learn by *doing*, by *thinking*, and by *social interaction.*

Learning styles are fact, not theory, and they are hardwired, so no matter how hard you try, you cannot change a student's learning style.

Learning by Doing

If you're one who learns "by doing," you would learn most effectively by working with a weapons instructor who does not just "explain," but rather gives the first simple steps to carry out and then allows you to begin independently carrying out those steps, one by one. The instructor should correct any mistakes as you go along, and as each step is conducted correctly, he would add additional steps and complexity as required.

Students taught in this manner are not as interested in the theory behind the training, and if given enough time and practice, the students will often develop the theory by themselves.

Learning by Thinking

Some people learn by understanding the theory and the background behind a given skill. When learning by this method, be sure to ask specific questions so that you understand the concepts in detail. For example, if asking a question about point-shooting distances, you'd want to ask in a way so that the answer would include specific guidelines on measurements, and explanation of why you'd transition to front sight focus at different distances, light conditions, size of threat, number of threats, etc. Without this conceptual information beforehand, a student who learns best by thinking would not be able grasp the concept of what is being taught.

Learning by Social Interaction

Some learn best by being part of a small training group. They enjoy the interaction, and learn best by observing their own peers conducting the activity. Simply watching the instructor carry out the activity does not reinforce the skill like practicing and discussing with others in their group. Isolated from interaction with peers, this student has great difficulty in transferring the offered knowledge into something they can carry out themselves. Based on learning research, learning by social interaction is generally a very effective way for female students to learn.

Given the differences in learning styles, the solution for weapons and tactics trainers is to train all students by utilizing methods that cover all of the learning style requirements. In training new shooters the presentation skills and actually understanding the "how" of training requires a great deal of study and applied thinking. I have seen many great shooters who are terrible instructors because they did not address these various learning styles.

Visual, Auditory, and Kinesthetic Learning

In conjunction with the above learning styles, people also learn in various degrees through visual, auditory, or kinesthetic stimuli. Visual people do well with Power Point slides, photos, graphs, demonstrations, etc. Most people fall into this group. Auditory learners rely on hearing, theory and specific details (often the "learning by thinking" group). And kinesthetic people learn by actually performing the skill (the "learning by doing" people).

TRAINING FUNDAMENTALS

"Using a firearm for defense implies reaction to an existing threat and not an initiation of an action. Therefore, the most crucial elements of defensive training are quick, reflexive gun-handling and mental control. While marksmanship training is certainly necessary, it must be combined with tactics. No one can guarantee perfect hits under stress, so training should not emphasize this aspect to the exclusion of the others. Reflexive gun-handling and mental control will leave your mind free to concentrate on shot placement and tactics."

—Louis Awerbuck

The Range Effect—A Deadly Syndrome

Always keep in mind that shooting ranges are typically supervised, controlled, unobstructed, and safe. The real world is not.

Range targets are typically unidirectional, non personal, and nonthreatening. Real world threats are not.

> **Training Tip:** Law enforcement officers and military personnel are duty-bound to confront certain situations head on. In contrast, the private citizen can and should retreat from potentially dangerous encounters whenever possible. If you belong to the latter group, your best option for personal security is a commitment to avoidance, deterrence, and de-escalation.

While we try to design our range training to be as "practical" and "tactical" as possible, it does not and cannot ever fully duplicate real-world confrontations. Always keep this in mind when training.

The responsible use of a weapon for self-defense is a multi-faceted subject that goes far beyond the simplistic notion of just pointing a weapon at a bad guy and pulling the trigger until he is dead. Weapons training requires professionalism, dedication, motivation, and a great deal of serious study. Self-defense handgun encounters aren't typically complicated, but they are unforgiving of arrogance, recklessness, ignorance, carelessness, or neglect.

Always take a tactical approach toward your training. Do not look at training as an administrative burden. There's a good feeling in knowing you're properly prepared for the threats of today's world.

Training the Mind and Body

Weapons and tactics training require 100 percent of your concentration. You must prepare yourself mentally before and during training. Do not train with weapons if you cannot have your mind 100 percent on the training. Not only can this be extremely dangerous, but it will also develop poor habits, which become ingrained into your subconscious mind.

The world's greatest shooters regularly dry practice. I highly suggest you do the same. It teaches and reinforces the draw stroke, weapons

> **Training Tip:** Do not bring pressure or stress to the range.

> **Training Tip:** Do not let performance anxiety get the best of you on the range.
>
> You need to be able to draw, fire, and handle your weapon reflexively. If you have to stop and think about your actions, you are in trouble.
>
> Good athletic ability, especially hand-eye coordination, is a real plus to good shooting but not essential to good shooting.

handling, trigger control, sighted techniques, reloads, malfunction clearing, etc.

Once you begin getting your techniques smooth, only then should you begin to add speed drills. Do not add in speed to your drills until you are smooth at conducting them. A timer, mandatory gear for professional and committed shooters, is a great training aid.

In a life-threatening situation you will do what you have trained yourself to do. You will do what you know will work. As previously discussed, the conscious mind does not work well at time of stress but the subconscious does. The subconscious, or nonanalytical portion of the mind, is influenced by a great deal of repetitive training. You will fight like you have trained, so train like you will fight. Repetition is the mother of all skills.

The "fight or flight" effects experienced during a life and death encounter are so pronounced that you will only perform at approximately 50 percent of your normal level. Under life-threatening stress, blood pressure will increase and your heart rate will increase, possibly up over 140 beats per minute. Most, if not all of your fine motor skills will deteriorate almost instantly, making the precision of gun handling and manipulation much more

> **Training Tip:** As you practice, work on one variable at a time. For example, concentrate on seeing the sight throughout the recoil cycle or focus on trigger reset and prep.

Training Tip: Don't dwell on poor shots, but learn from them.

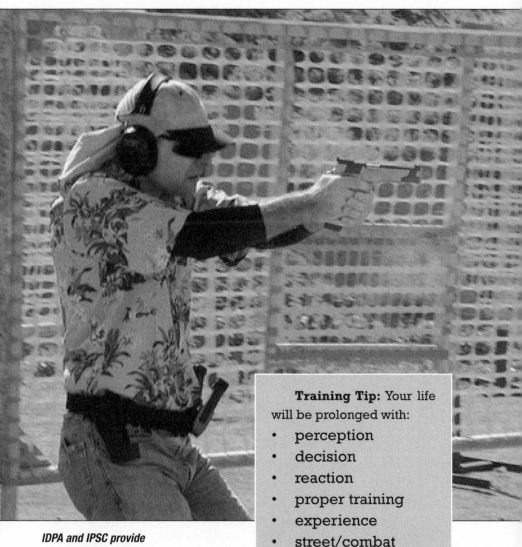

IDPA and IPSC provide incredible training opportunities.

Training Tip: Your life will be prolonged with:

- perception
- decision
- reaction
- proper training
- experience
- street/combat wisdom
- proper mind-set
- good instincts

Training Tip: Develop a positive attitude. You can shoot just as well as the next person if you try hard enough. You may not be as gifted in hand-eye coordination, etc., but with extra effort you can become an excellent shot.

It takes one repetition to learn a technique. It takes approximately 1,500-3,000 repetitions to assure programmed response of complex psychomotor skills become reflexive.

If the shooter has too many choices and has not mentally prepared an option, response time will be longer.

Training Tip: Dry practice with an empty weapon provides some of the best training. You get plenty of reflex-building repetition; dry firing allows you to develop trigger manipulation skills without flinch-inducing noise and recoil. Be sure to simulate trigger reset with each trigger press.

difficult. And you may also develop tunnel vision and your hearing may become distorted, a condition called auditory exclusion (temporary deafness).

It is very important to learn and know what effects you will experience when in the fight or flight mode. Everyone reacts differently and it is extremely important to experience these signs and symptoms during scenario-based training the first time rather than in a real life confrontation.

Defensive shooting is an art based on a science, which is based on principles and techniques. Target identification, short time intervals, high-stress situations, different environmental conditions, differing numbers of threats and non-threats, situational awareness, and many other factors are all intrinsic parts of defensive shooting training.

When training always remain in a tactical mind-set. Be certain your training and tactics are based on the real world, rather than being competitive or theoretically based. And, for your sake, your family's sake, your partner's sake,

Author (right) conducting some tactical defensive training with fellow weapons and tactics instructor Jim C.

Training Tip: The majority of law enforcement deaths in the United States occur within three meters, three shots, and three rounds. Ninety-one percent of U.S. law enforcement engagements are within 20 feet, 67 percent are within 10 feet, and the average engagement time is 2.5 seconds. And 80 percent of deaths occurred during the hours of darkness.

etc., do all you can to hone your skills and your combat mind-set to the maximum degree possible.

Suggested Training Plan

Below is a training plan similar to what is used by many successful weapons and tactics trainers throughout the defensive shooting community. It is effective because it addresses the various learning

Training Tip: If handgun presentation, rapid indexing of target, and compressed surprise break are not aspects of your training, you will most likely be in grave danger during a real world confrontation.

Training Tip: During your training strive for developing "economy of movement."

An Indonesian martial arts adage states, "Repetition is the mother of skill." Practice makes habits. Only perfect practice makes perfect. Pay attention to detail during all of your training sessions.

styles discussed in the previous chapter. This may be a plan you want to incorporate as a self-taught student or when training others.

Level One

Level One includes two types of training: insight development instruction and defensive shooting skills.

Insight development is accomplished by using audio-visual instructional aids, i.e., home-defense training videos, listening and watching interviews conducted by those who survived deadly encounters, al-Qaeda training videos, law enforcement re-enactments, actual footage with threats, Power Point presentations, graphs, charts, etc.

Defensive skill drills utilize methodically well-thought-out lesson plans with corresponding dry and live-fire drills that range from weapons safety to combat mind-set to basic marksmanship drills, to tactics up through the use of deadly force.

"For ten years, I trained like a man possessed. My practice regimen included not only shooting an incredible number of rounds, but also thousands of hours of dry training at home. If I was not working on my gun or loading ammo, I was dry firing. My cross-training included running, weight training, martial arts, yoga, meditation, and constant reading of anything I thought might help. Over the next years, I won the Bianchi Cup in 1983 and '84, the Masters in 1989, and was a five-time member of the Sportsman's Team Challenge national championship team. I've qualified for the United States IPSC Gold Team every year since 1983, and twice finished second at the Steel Challenge, SOF, and the IPSC U.S. Open Nationals."

—Brian Enos

Level Two

Visualized interaction is ideally initially conducted under the direction of a trainer and then the student progresses through self-training. Visualized interaction consists of visualization and judgment training using audio-visual training simulators and computerized training programs. By using simple visualization, the trainee thinks-out and visualizes solutions to given scenarios.

Level Three

The goal of level-three training—in which *unconscious competence* is strengthened—is to replicate as closely as possible the encounters you might experience. This is done through proper role-playing exercises, force-on-force drills, the use of real or close-to-real weapons that fire non-lethal projectiles, role players that shoot, move, take

cover, and communicate, and problem-solving scenario-based training.

The role players, both threats and non-threats, must all understand the objectives and importance of the training being conducted. Too often this training turns into a free-for-all game. This training must be conducted professionally since it is building the trainee's subconscious mind, on which his life may depend someday.

This type of training is typically done with scenario-based exercises such as: shoot-house scenarios, red-gun exercises, and force-on-force training with Simunitions, paintball, or air-soft training guns.

The shoot-house scenarios and force-on-force exercises should be interactive and have threats and non-threats that respond with both movement and verbal communication to the actions of the trainee. They should also introduce stimuli that are distracting and extraneous to the scenario, such as low light, smoke, non-threats screaming and crying, loud music, etc.

> **Training Tip:**
> Awareness = Distance, Distance = Time, and Time = Life.

Red-gun and force-on-force scenario-based training are some of the most effective forms of multi-stimulus, problem-solving scenario-based training available. They offer increased consequences, either through reinforcement or by punishment; for instance, if the trainee makes a mistake in evaluating the situation, he may be "assaulted or shot".

Simunitions, paintball and air-soft weapons add an additional level of consequence above simple red-gun training. The impacts they deliver are a clear reminder that the trainee has done something wrong. Conversely, escaping a difficult situation or defeating a threat that shoots back gives one a sense of emotional satisfaction that is highly reinforcing. Force-on-force training doesn't just build good habits, it ingrains them.

Level-three scenarios should be constructed so that they are equal to or only slightly above the current skill level of the trainee. The scenarios must challenge but not overwhelm the trainee. If the scenario is too far beyond the trainee's ability, then the trainee may become traumatized, develop a lack of self-confidence, and simply give up on developing the skills. This could have serious

> **Training Tip:** Move laterally or at an oblique angle to get off-line.
> In a violent confrontation, prowess combined with combat accuracy will contribute to your survival.

Weapons and tactics instructor showing how it is done

potential consequences if the trainee becomes involved in an incident involving deadly force.

Tactical Guidelines

"God made some men big and some men small, and Sam Colt made 'em equal."—Old West saying

Tactics, as defined by the weapons community, includes a wide range of interpretations, all of which contribute to our modern understanding. These include:

- The skillful manipulation of time and distance so that you get the advantage and the threat does not.
- The art and science of using the available means to achieve an end.
- "Common sense applied with the specific knowledge of the involved discipline."—Mas Ayoob
- "The actions you take in furtherance of your particular goal, with your options frequently constrained by the mission, opponent, resources, environment and time available."—Former Secret Service agent and National Tactical Invitational Shootist Gary Wistrand

Other than your combat mind-set, nothing will help you become better or more effective at defense than improving your weapons tactics. Neither this book, nor any book, can list all tactics that cover all situations, but I have provided some general guidelines, principles, and tips. Tactics have to be created for the situation and the environment, often on the fly. This chapter outlines some basic guidelines you should consider when discussing, drafting, reviewing or practicing defensive tactics.

That said, home, vehicle, or workplace tactics, when carrying vs. not carrying, in a bad part of town or in a war zone—all differ greatly. Tactics that police use in Philadelphia are strikingly different than those used in Sedona. Tactics being used by our military in Iraq differ vastly from what were used in Vietnam. As well they should. Like anything, tactics evolve.

As General Douglas MacArthur put it: "It was close; but that's the way it is in war. You win or lose, live or die—and the difference is just an eyelash."

Think of tactics as tools you have available in your tactical toolbox. Picking the right tool for the right job is critical; for instance you wouldn't use a screwdriver when you need a sledge hammer.

The effective deployment of tactics will provide "leverage" during a confrontation. Having a wide range of tactics at your disposal maximizes the probability that you will select a suitable course of action.

> **Training Tip:** Smaller targets are harder to hit. Moving targets are much harder to hit. Targets shooting back are hardest to hit. Be all three!
>
> Never lose sight of your threat.

How you respond in a gunfight depends on a number of factors. In a perfect world, avoidance, de-escalation, and seeking immediate cover or concealment may be your best choice of tactics. But, since we do not live in a perfect world, we must plan and be ready to do more.

SWAT and military tactical training.

Training Tip: Your No. 1 option for personal security is a lifelong commitment to:
- Avoidance
- Deterrence
- De-escalation

Photos courtesy of GTI

Factors to consider

- Where is the closest available cover/concealment?
- Where is your weapon and in what condition is it in?
- How close is the threat?
- What does the threat have as a weapon?
- Are the rounds the threat is firing effective?
- Are other non-threats in the immediate vicinity?
- Are you adept at controlling the physical responses to stress?

Training Tip: Concealment keeps you from being seen. Cover keeps you from being hit. Cover is better.

This is good concealment—it is not cover.

Shooter taking advantage of good concealment

Neither I nor any other shooting instructor can say, "You must always do it this way" or "You must never do it that way." If we told you this, we would all be wrong some of the time. You may be point-shooting at the target that is within 10 feet or taking the well-aimed shot to return fire at the target who is 20 yards back or more. I cannot profess that in a real world situation when confronted by a threat, you always need to point-shoot or always take the well-aimed shot, because I would be wrong in some of the situations. There are no absolutes—"situation dictates."

The decision on how to respond is yours and it must be based on your training, experience, and the situation as you perceive it. Generally speaking, you must neutralize the threat more quickly at close ranges than at longer ranges. And keep in mind that it will normally take several seconds for a determined attacker to be stopped by even the most precisely delivered handgun rounds.

Tactics are never absolute and all can be modified and improvised. In the military we used Standard Operating Procedures (SOPs), which "are written in blood," and tactics for almost every circumstance and condition imaginable. We practiced them regularly. The tactics change depending on the geographical location, e.g., the jungles of the Philippines, the arctic conditions of Alaska, the river systems of Central America, the urban settings of the Middle East or the Balkans. The tactics change depending on the *Rules of Engagement (ROEs)*, the political stability/instability of the region, and the current threat level.

Our SOPs and tactics change regularly and evolve. As tactics evolve, some get compromised and become ineffective with time. As a member of the military or police force it is up to you to stay as current as possible. Anyone interested in personal defense should watch the news, read law enforcement accounts of the activities in your own community, and develop home and workplace tactics. Teach your family how to develop a combat mind-set and the tactics they need to protect themselves.

Photos courtesy of GTI

> **Training Tip:** A person running at full speed can cover up to 10 yards per second. It takes an average of two seconds to draw and fire an accurate shot.

Visualization

Tactics training does not require a range or a shooting house to develop or practice. They can be practiced within the mind through

visualization, a very effective training aid. Simply put, you need to know what to do if X, Y, or Z happens. Have a plan. If I am in my home and it is broken into, I will do this … If I am at the ATM machine and a person comes up close to me, I will do this.

Photos courtesy of GTI

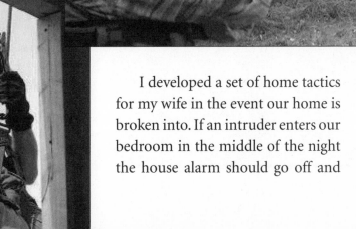

I developed a set of home tactics for my wife in the event our home is broken into. If an intruder enters our bedroom in the middle of the night the house alarm should go off and

Training Tip: You need to be able to defend yourself because when seconds count, the cops are normally minutes away.

It is important to have a "SAFE" (safe area for evacuation) in your home and workplace. The SAFE place should provide cover or at least concealment, a flashlight, a phone, and of course a weapon.

the dogs should start barking well before anyone enters the house. But in the event the intruder does make it to the bedroom door, she is to roll out of bed, using the bed as concealment and hold her .357 Magnum at the mid-center of the door (approximately mid-center of

> **Training Tip:** Move away from your threat, get reactive distance, get off-line (lateral and diagonal movements are preferred) and take cover.

a man's chest). She is also within arm's reach of the home phone, a cell phone, and a flashlight. She has two options: to blind the intruder with the Sure Fire flashlight while aiming center mass and give the intruder the option to freeze and get on the ground. Or, if she determines the person is a threat, she is to neutralize the threat. This would require her to shoot until the intruder is no longer a threat. Her .357 Magnum is a 7-shot revolver. If she requires more than seven .357 rounds to neutralize the threat, she has a shotgun loaded with buck shot within a few steps of the bed. Once the shooting is over, she will hold cover on the lifeless threat and call 911.

If you find yourself in a situation where you have to search for a threat that may be in your home or workspace, for example, scan in and out, rather than left and right, and watch out for the tendency to be visually drawn back to objects that you've already identified as non-threats. The subconscious mind plays tricks on us when in life-threatening situations, so we tend to try and calm down by repeatedly looking at something we know won't hurt us. Don't assume anything. Don't turn your back on any thing or any area you haven't checked out first. Try to keep your back toward a wall or a cleared area when moving. It is easier in the low-light environment for a threat to slip unnoticed into a previously searched area.

> **Training Tip:** Be aggressive and quick with your defensive actions.

Try to remain quiet as long as possible and not give your position

> **Training Tip:** If you are not shooting in a gunfight, you should be communicating, reloading, and/or moving to cover.

away. Don't scrape your back against a wall or drag your feet when moving. These are typical things people do under stress.

Try to maximize the distance between yourself and potential threats and any potential danger areas as much as possible. Your best defense against danger is distance, cover, and concealment.

Keep your balance and your ability to remain mobile. This allows for forward, backward, right, and left movement.

When using force against a threat, your survival depends on your actions before, during, and after the application of your tactics. Unfortunately, many people drop their guard before it is safe to do so. A failure to follow-through and/or scan appropriately can get you killed.

Darkness can be your friend. In low-light environments you may remain undetected longer, you may be able to flee the area undetected, and your tactics may be more effective, especially if you can maintain the "element of surprise" over a threat.

When a round hits a hard, flat surface at any angle, the round will tend to bounce off and travel six to eight inches parallel to the surface. These are called skip rounds. Keep this in mind in houses, buildings, parking lots, near hoods of cars, etc. This is one of the reasons tactical teams stay off of the walls when moving in a house or building. The worst shot in the world can be lucky by simply shooting at a wall or the ground and allowing his skip rounds to hit you.

> **Training Tip:** Bullet impacts are usually not visible on clothing.

If possible, stay behind cover or move from cover to cover. Law enforcement studies show over 80 percent of U.S. police officers injured or killed did not use available cover. If you have an opportunity to take cover or concealment—take it . . . but always remember that cover and concealment are only temporary.

Do not give away your position with noise, lights, or by leading your movement with your weapon.

Shooting Maxims

The Tactical Principle: There will be no time to "get ready."

"You have to "be ready," or be prepared to accept murder/ mayhem at the hands of enemy who will sometimes cross paths with you, no matter how careful and foresighted you try to be!"
—Anonymous

"It's not the will to win that matters–everyone has that. It's the will to *prepare* to win that matters."
—Paul "Bear" Bryant

"Failure is good when training—without it we would be lazy and wouldn't motivate ourselves to change. Look at failure as an opportunity to improve."
—Brian Enos

"Move quickly, shoot carefully."
—Peter Samish

"An amateur trains until he gets it right. A professional trains until he can't get it wrong."
—Author unknown

"You will not rise to the occasion but you will default to your level of training. Practice perfect practice!"
—Barrett Tillman

If you encounter a threat and he is wise enough to surrender, keep your distance from him. You should be in condition red. Take and keep control of the situation. If he tries anything, you must be

ready to defend yourself. Have him place his weapon on the floor and kick it out of his reach. Then, have him kneel down, cross his ankles, and have him put his head on the ground or toward a wall while placing his hands with fingers interlaced behind his neck. Do your best to not let him see you or communicate with you.

Keep your weapon pointed at the threat. Once he is secured and immobile, go to the ready position. Give him directions in a clear, concise, controlled manner, without yelling. Stay in control and let him know that you are confident and in charge of the situation.

When law enforcement arrives, try not to be in a situation that might be construed as you being a threat. More than one defensive shooter has been mistakenly shot by appearing to be the "bad guy." Remember that police officers don't know who you are or what the circumstances are; they cannot afford to take chances.

To avoid this potential problem, many law enforcement agencies will now keep you on the telephone until the responding officers arrive, all the while having you communicate information to them while they're in transit. This is for your protection as well as theirs—the more they know about the event, and your physical description, the better. But do not let the phone call take you from your duty of covering this threat.

Many defensive weapons tacticians have devoted their lives to the study of tactics and yet never came close to knowing all there is to know, let alone keeping up with this ever-changing discipline. Nonetheless, if you apply sound tactics the odds of your survival will greatly increase if and when you are confronted by a threat(s). You will gain an overwhelming advantage if you combine the application of sound tactics with a finely tuned combat mind-set and current marksmanship training.

SHOOTING DRILLS

"Start and end every shooting session with precision shots just to remind yourself that you can do it, and to have a feeling of balance and accuracy going into the more speed-oriented shooting."

—Brian Enos

Basic marksmanship fundamentals need to be developed, reviewed, and practiced regularly. No matter how experienced you are, it is essential to go through the basic fundamentals and tactics through visualization, dry fire and live fire, and practicing perfect practice, prior to training at more advanced levels.

Below are some shooting drills practiced by many military, government, and sport shooters. It's imperative that your techniques do not suffer when adding speed to your drills. With all drills, the object is to be smooth and "smooth is fast."

Once you can complete the drills without sacrificing technique then add speed. As many serious shooters do you can also simulate how your body will function during the fight-or-flight mode, by doing any of the following drills after doing 20 or so good push-ups and/or running before shooting.

John Shaw and Brian Enos battling it out.

Once the marksmanship fundamentals have been reviewed and practiced, then you are ready to move on to drills that include: shooting from cover; shooting off-hand with the dominant and non-dominant hands; shooting from the various positions and at different distances; and shooting while moving.

I like to tell my students that we are taking the "crawl, walk, run" approach to training. Initially every step is performed slowly and with perfection. Once the students begin to look smooth with their movements, we then put a bit of time pressure on them.

Do not rush into any complex or advanced training. You need a very solid foundation before adding in speed or complexity to your training routine.

"In practice, tell yourself to become aware of something that you are not normally aware of. Pick a drill—then repeat the same drill over an over an over, while just watching to 'see what you see.' If you can do this—just watch the activity with no preconceived notions or any regard as to the outcome—you may see or realize something extraordinary."

—Brian Enos

When you go to the range to practice, have a set of drills you want to work on. Don't just go to the range and send lead down range. Most importantly, practice skills that are needed in real world confrontations. Don't waste a lot of time practicing skills you will never need. For the most part, the average shooter needs to work on quickly getting the weapon into action from concealment and combat accuracy.

"It is a good idea to keep up with your progress over a period of time. Keep a log of the drills you practice and your accuracy rate, so you can compare it to what

Training Tip: End all shooting sessions by shooting slow fire groups into an eight-inch group at 25 yards.

Kelly Armenta, weapons instructor with the South Carolina Law Enforcement Division.
Photos courtesy of Richard Belmore, South Carolina Law Enforcement Division

you do at a later day. Otherwise, it's difficult to know if you are improving."

—Robbie Robinson

Targets

When shooting paper targets try to use either funny-face targets or IPSC targets. If you do not have either use a sheet of 8.5" x 11" paper which is the same height and just slightly wider than the A-zone of an IPSC target and very close to what is regarded as "combat accuracy."

Combat Accuracy Drills

Simply engage relatively small moving targets that are exposed for only .25–.75 of a second from various distances using a Protimer. Turning targets work really well for this exercise.

Competitive shooting drills

Cover Drills

From the 3–5 yard lines:
- Begin by using standing cover, then kneeling, and then prone.
- Progress to briskly walking and then to running to cover and then firing.

- Include tactical reloads and malfunction drills before changing profile.
- All hits should be in the combat accuracy zone.
- Train using both right- and left-side cover.
- Change shooting profiles from standing to kneeling, kneeling to standing, standing to prone, etc.

- 1 rd/3 sec
- 2 rds/3 sec
- 3 rds/3 sec

Move to Cover—Tactical and Speed Reload Drill

From the 10 yard line:
- Move to cover (right side barricade), fire three rounds center mass, tactical reload, change profile, fire three additional rounds center mass.
- Repeat on left side barricade.
- Repeat utilizing standing, kneeling, and prone positions.
- Repeat shooting center mass and head shots.
- With each additional drill, include dummy rounds (for malfunction practice) and use partial magazines for speed and tactical reload practices.
- Begin by utilizing single static targets and as you progress, advance to: multiple static targets; single moving targets; multiple moving targets; and then intermix threat and non-threat targets.

Malfunction Drills

From the 7, 10 and 15 yard lines:
- Stand from 7 yards, knee from 10 yards, and prone from 15 yards.
- Load an entire magazine for each position with two to three pieces of brass or dummy rounds in each, with the rest of the rounds being live.
- Shoot three to four rounds from behind cover into the combat accuracy zone and one to the head. Take cover and repeat.

Trigger Reset Drills

- Dry fire—concentrate on trigger reset.

- Dry fire—concentrate on all fundamentals, but have your partner rack your weapon, trigger reset.

Rapid Fire Shooting Drills

From the 5 and 10 yard lines:

Keeping all rounds in the combat accuracy zone, see how many times you can rapidly make all of the shots effective. Have your partner count how many pieces of brass remain in the air at the same

time (three in the air at one time is impressive!). A good shooter will keep all rounds in the 8-inch combat accuracy zone from 10 feet and have five pieces of brass in the air at the same time.

Pivot Drills

From the 5 and 10 yard lines:
- Pivot 90 degrees toward the target. Practice from the left and the right.
- Pivot 180 degrees toward the target. Practice turning to the left and to the right.
- First snap your head toward target, then pivot while drawing. Practice this one- and two-handed.
- Also practice this from the hip and from the standing-pivot to kneeling positions.
- Fire three to five rounds to center mass and one to head with each pivot.

Farnam's Drill

From the 7 yard line:
- Developed by John Farnam, renowned weapons instructor.
- Load six live rounds and one dummy round. The dummy should not be the first or last round, nor should it be the round in the

chamber. Fire six center-mass shots, clearing the dummy with a "tap, rack, assess" when it comes up. Then reload and fire two head shots.

Advanced—Combined Skill-Set Drills

From the 7 and 15 yard lines:

Position	Distance	Number of Rounds	Time	Drill
Standing	7yds	5rds	1.5sec	one shot each draw
	10yds	5rds	2.0sec	one shot each draw
	15yds	5rds	2.5sec	one shot each draw
	25yds 5rds		5.0sec	one shot each draw from
Kneeling from behind barricade	7yds	10rds	2.5sec	2 shots each draw
	10yds	10rds	2.5sec	2 shots each draw
	10yds	10rds	6.0sec	multiple targets, one shot, reload, one shot
	10yds	20rds	8.0sec	2 shots, one target,
Standing position	10yds	12rds	4.0sec	from ready position, Mozambique (2 shots center mass, 1 to the head) while advancing to the threat

Bill Drill

From the 7 yard line:
• Developed by Bill Wilson.

- Draw and fire six rounds. The string does not count unless every round hits the combat accuracy zone. An IPSC Grandmaster can do this consistently in less than three seconds. The Bill Drill is good for developing your ability to see and shoot quickly.
- Goal: under 2 seconds

Perfect Shot Drill

From the 25 yard line:

- From the ready position, fire a single round in less than 3 seconds twenty-five consecutive times. To achieve this, everything must be perfect. You must keep all 25 rounds in the combat accuracy zone.

IPSC Semi Handgun Qualification Course

From the 7 yard line:

First Stage:	6 rds in 3 seconds or less (x 6)
Second Stage:	2 rds in 4 seconds or less (x 6)
Third Stage:	6 rds in 10 seconds or less (x 6)

From the 10 yard line:

First Stage:	1 rd in 3 seconds or less (x 6)
Second Stage:	2 rds in 4 seconds or less (x 6)
Third Stage:	6 rds, reload, fire 6 additional rounds in 30 seconds or less.

From the 15 yard line:

First Stage: 6 rounds from the kneeling position; reload while moving to second firing position (left cover), fire 6 rounds; reload, move to third position (right cover), fire 6 rounds. Clear and holster in 2 minutes or less.

Accuracy Drills

- Begin by shooting small (1–3 inch diameter) dots from 3 yards
- Progress to shooting 6-inch circles from 7 yards.
- Practice the draw stroke, ready position, multiple shots on one target, transition between target, one-handed aimed fire, reloads, and malfunction corrections.

Accuracy and Speed Drills

From the 3–5 yard lines:
- Fire 6 rounds at the first 8-inch circle at a shot per second.
- Then shoot a separate string of 6 at a second 8-inch circle at a half-second per shot.
- Zero misses and at least 50 percent hits in the combat accuracy zone is a good minimum standard.

Dozier Drill

This is an excellent drill for multiple target practice. It simulates a response to the multiple terrorists who kidnapped NATO General Dozier in Italy.

From the 5 and 10 yard lines:
- This drill is typically shot on five steel "pepper popper" or head-plate targets.
- Space the targets at random intervals and ranges.
- All "pepper popper" shots are to be in the combat accuracy zone.

Precision Shooting Drill

Shooting from a pistol rest or a bench rest will help develop and improve acquiring a sight picture, proper trigger control, and confidence that your weapon shoots to point of aim.

Shooting from a pistol or bench rest is an excellent way for a shooter to observe the shooting process (watching the front sight rise and fall, the slide operate, and the weapon come back into battery and on target).

Place ¼" dots on a sheet of paper. Fire one shot per dot at 7 yards; bullet must break the edge to score.

Slow Fire Accuracy Drills

- Place a 1" target dot on a blank sheet of paper.
- Begin at 7 yds and progress to 25 yds.
- Load only one round into the magazine or cylinder.
- Slow fire (no time limit) practicing "perfect practice."
- After every shot, holster and step off line.

The Receding Bullseyes Drill

- Place 1.5" target dot on a blank sheet of paper at the 1 yard line.
- It should be relatively easy to put your rounds straight dead center into the bullseye.
- Fire 3 rounds.
- Move back to the 2 yard line and fire 3 rounds.
- Move back to the 3–10 yard lines (in yard increments).
- You should notice that you can "lock on" to the bullseye by doing this, to the point where you can shoot a tight group at longer distances than normal.
- You should also become aware of the shooting factors that degrade accuracy.

Ball and Dummy Drill

- When the trigger is pulled on a weapon during slow fire, the weapon should not jerk or move.
- The sights should stay aligned on target while your eyes remain focused on the front sight.
- If the weapon does jerk it is because you anticipated the shot.
- Load your magazines mixing live rounds with dummy rounds or empty brass. For a revolver, leave one or more chambers empty.
- As you slow fire concentrate on keeping the weapon steady and the sights on target.

- When the dummy round/brass cap comes up you will definitely notice any jerking.
- Keep your sights aligned and on target while you release the trigger just enough to re-engage the sear (proper follow-through).
- If you have a laser or optical sight, it's even more difficult to keep the dot perfectly on the target when the dummy round or brass comes up.

No Blinking Drill

Most shooters blink involuntarily when they fire a weapon. This is due to the noise or anticipated noise of shooting. When a shooter blinks, he can't be watching the sights through recoil for a good follow-through, and has to reacquire the visual index on the sight before firing the next shot.

As Brian Enos said, "This is a fundamental barrier to advanced shooting; you can't have a fast visual control of the gun if you aren't watching the sight through recoil."

To help in keeping relaxed, try to keep your facial muscles relaxed while shooting. Work with dominant and non-dominant hand shooting. Concentrate on keeping your eyes open for the complete cycle. After you have achieved the ability to relax and keep your eyes open, you will notice a tremendous increase in awareness.

Correcting Trigger Slap Drill

Many novice shooters remove their trigger finger completely off the trigger between shots when shooting rapid fire. This is ineffi-cient since it not only takes more time but it leads to inaccurate shooting because of the tendency to slap the trigger on the subse-quent shots.

To correct this be sure to follow-through with each shot by holding the trigger back all the way through recoil. When the sights are again aligned slowly release the trigger until the link re-engages. Then press to make the next shot.

Shooting with Both Eyes Open

Many shooters close or squint their non-dominant eye in order to focus on the front sight. As we know, doing so impairs peripheral vision, depth perception, and increases eye fatigue. Target-to-target transitions are much quicker when both eyes are open while shooting.

Place a piece of scotch tape or smear Vaseline on your shooting glasses over your non-dominant eye and learn to shoot with both eyes open. The tape or Vaseline will obscure the non-dominant eye's picture to the point where it will not interfere with your sight picture. Shoot with both eyes open while watching the sight through the recoil process.

Sight Acquisition Drill

- Useful for training at target identification.
- From the low ready position.
- The low ready position provides the shooter a complete field of vision while enabling him to get the weapon quickly on target if required.
- The low ready position keeps the weapon low enough to see over it.

ACKNOWLEDGMENTS »

I am indebted to the many combat shooters—from the military services and those in various U.S. government agencies, the law enforcement community and to the countless professional shooting instructors—who have inspired me and taught me the importance of sound and professional weapons and tactics training.

I conducted a great deal of research and spent more than 12 years on this project. I re-examined my long-held assumptions about training and was very methodical in my research. However this project would not have been possible without the enormous amount assistance I received from my wife, Dawn. Dawn's journalism background was invaluable in putting the smooth touches and final edit on the MDG manuscript. My good friend, not to mention one of the most professional gunslingers I have ever had the privilege to work with, Dick Conger also provided incredible technical input to the text. And finally, professional writer and editor Devon O'Neal provided a clear and concise edit to the text.

ABOUT THE AUTHOR »

Don Mann's impressive military biography includes being a Navy SEAL, a decorated combat veteran, a Special Operations Technician, and a Combat Medic. He also served as a Program Manager and Lead Instructor in Jungle, Desert and Arctic Survival, Small Arms and Foreign Weapons/Tactics, as well as Survival, Evasion, Resistance and Escape (SERE) training. Don currently lives in Williamsburg, VA. Learn more about Don at www.usfrogmann.com.

INDEX

NOTES